THE HOBDAY CONNECTION

THE HOBDAY CONNECTION

*A Story Of War, Love, Hate, Intrigue, Deception
And A Search For The Truth.*

DANE HOBDAY HAYS

authorHOUSE®

AuthorHouse™
1663 Liberty Drive
Bloomington, IN 47403
www.authorhouse.com
Phone: 1-800-839-8640

First published by AuthorHouse   11/23/2011

ISBN: 978-1-4685-0214-5 (sc)
ISBN: 978-1-4685-0213-8 (ebk)

Printed in the United States of America

CONTENTS

THIS BOOK IS DEDICATED

TO THE MEN & WOMEN OF THE US MILITARY SERVICES PAST & PRESENT. ESPECIALLY TO THE CREW OF B-29 TAIL#44-86343, OF THE 19TH BOMB GROUP AT KADENA AFB, SHOT DOWN OVER KOREA ON 13 SEPTEMBER 1952. AND TO ARMY CPL JOHN A. SPRUELL, 57th FIELD ARTILLERY, WHO DIED AT THE CHOSIN RESERVOIR, ON 6 DECEMBER 1950 AND TO THE REMAINING SURVIVORS OF THAT DREADFUL BATTLE, NOW KNOWN AS THE CHOSIN FEW.

Special Thanks to Fred Parker, Frank Farrell, The Chosin Few Association, Robert Crawford, Ed Moynagh, Chuck & Marilyn Haley, Bruce Salisbury, Bill Aseere, Ray Vallowe, Dennis Spruell, Marian Fischer, Major General Mason Whitney, Phil O'Brien, Wayland Mayo, Frank Nagy, Eugene Hill, Rance Farrell & The AUSA, JPAC/DPMO Offices, JB Wiles, Members of the 307th Bomb Wing, Ted Barker & The Korean War Project. Without their encouragement, support, guidance and assistance this story would never have been told.

PREFACE

This is a historical biography, all of the characters and events are true. The portrayals of public figures mentioned in this book are accurate and true. There has been no intention to harm or cause embarrassment to any person alive or dead, the similarity of names being purely coincidental.

RESEARCH CREDITS

Departments of the Defense Air Force, Marine, and Army National Archives

Montezuma-Cortez High School & Cortez City Library, Cortez, CO

"Chosin, Heroic Ordeal of the Korean War", Eric Hammel—Zenith Press1981

"Breakout, The Chosin Reservoir Campaign", Martin Russ—Penguin Books 1999

"The Korean War in Photos," Donald Goldstein & Harry Maihafer—Brassey's 2000

"Remembered Prisoners of a Forgotten War," Lewis Carlson—St. Martins Press 2002

"History of Air Education & Training Command 1942 to 2002",Office of History & Research, Randolph Air Force Base, US Gov. Printing Office 2005

"East of Chosin"—Lt. Col. Roy Appleman, 1987 Texas A&M University Press

"No Sweat". Frank (Bud) Farrell—1st Books/Author House 2005

"A Woman's Path"—Jo Giese

Credence Catholic Communications Publications

"The Unsung Hero East of the Chosin Reservoir", CPT John Labadini, US Army Air Defense Artillery School, Ft. Bliss, TX October 2000.

Ray Vallowe—Personal Memoirs, survivor of Chosin, 57th FA Bn.

Dane Hays—Personal Memoirs & Photo Collection

"Ava My Story"—Ava Gardner, Bantam Books, November 1990

"The Untold Story of Howard Hughes"—Peter H. Brown, Penguin Books USA 1996

FOREWORD

DANE HOBDAY HAYS' SUIHO ODYSSEY

"Our nation honors her sons and daughters who answered a call to defend a country they never knew and a people they never met." . . . . —Korean War Memorial—

To—Bud Farrell, from Dane Hobday Hays via email:
"How can I describe the feeling that I have, reading your email . . . You are the first person in 8 months of intensive internet & letters, that has responded regarding B29 Tail #44-86343, A1C Fred Parker, A1C Jimmie Hobday and all the rest. I received the records from St Louis, too late for this newsletter going out, to add the info that Jimmie Hobday went from B-29 Combat Crew Training at Randolph in Feb 52 to Lake Charles AFB then to HQ SQ 307th at MacDill on 11 May 52. Dane (Hobday) Hays"

On August 27th, 2008, four and one half years after publishing my own Korean War B-29 Combat Crew Memoir, "NO SWEAT", I received a 307th Bomb Wing Quarterly Newsletter and found within an article and the above inquiry by someone seeking information regarding a B-29 lost on September 13th, 1952, over The North Korean Suiho Hydroelectric Dam and Power plant on the Yalu River. In addition, there was a typical picture of a B-29 crew in front of a B-29 and my heart raced almost to bursting . . ."PARKER" . . . of my 1951 Gunnery School days! I knew it had to be a picture of Fred Parker's crew since they were the ONLY crew lost directly over Suiho that night, out of the 32 bombers crossing the target . . . AND immediately in front of our ship on the bomb run. I have related in greater detail regarding this incident in several "NO SWEAT" stories, but now there is a great deal more . . . strictly by remote chance and remaining between "people that have never met "!

In the picture, with no identification of crew members, and too small to really recognize individual features, I blurted out to myself

"PARKER", and I was certain that I could identify Fred Parker at the far left of the rear row . . . reasonably confirmed then with a small magnifying glass, and re-confirmed with the later receipt of a larger picture with names on the back, from the inquirer, Dane Hays then of Sedona, now in Prescott, Arizona.

In the newsletter below the picture, there was a request that "If anyone has personal knowledge of Airman First Class Hobday, 307th Bomb Group/Wing (1946—1954), OR of the incident referred to, please contact Dane Hays." I immediately emailed Dane Hays and related that I did have knowledge and in fact had written very extensively of the Suiho incident, and in fact had a close personal friend—the Right Gunner and ONLY survivor—aboard the very same aircraft in which Dane's father, Jimmy Hobday, the Tail Gunner, had been lost and as dreadfully observed by our crew. I received an almost immediate email response just after my first unsuccessful phone call to Dane Hays.

A slightly later phone call resulted in floods of emotion for both of us. With my finding a picture of Fred Parker after 56 years, and far more importantly, for Dane at 61 years of age, and a 19 year military career, seeking and now finally finding information regarding his "father" who had been lost with 10 others of the Parker crew in combat over the Yalu River before Dane was barely 5 years old . . . but in fact his "father" was lost to Dane at his very birth!

Dane and I have discussed his heritage and legacy and I encouraged HIM to write his memoir, while he has extended the very great courtesy to me of my "excerpting" some of the thoughts related to what MUST be HIS story . . . his life's journey and perhaps very belated but welcome, if not joyful, CLOSURE! I have been delighted and honored that Dane Hays has suggested that I have perhaps placed a few "keystones" in his very belated search for his "past," all because of his one more, and perhaps even very last exasperated inquiry.

That we are very close now, on August 29, 2008, to the 56th anniversary date of September 13th, 1952, and have only just now provided some answers, several so desperately needed by a "family" member of one of our long lost Korean War compatriots. I am once again reminded of the poignant tribute . . ."*Our nation honors her sons and daughters who answered a call to defend a country they never knew and a people they never met.*" . . . .—*Korean War Memorial*—

Paraphrasing that tribute, Dane's father, Jimmie Hobday, answered a call to defend a country he never knew and a people he never met . . . leaving a son he had by a love he could not keep . . . Dane now had a father and mother who were never again to be together, and yet never to be forgotten . . . Unlike "The Forgotten War", that had kept them all so far apart . . . Korea!

Then Jimmy Hobday, who had come to visit and frequently play in the yard with little Dane Hays, was lost to eternity. Apparently with his own youthful secrets taken too over the Suiho Hydroelectric Dam & Power plant on the Yalu River border of North Korea and Manchuria, China. Moreover, Dane Hays at two years of age and living just down the street from Jimmie Rowland Hobday's home, played in the yard, and only occasionally comforted by the love of and in his mother's lap.

A legacy recently burnished by a trip to Arlington National Cemetery with only the honored and resting soul of Jimmy Hobday and an inheritance of the favorable genes that permitted Dane Hays to rise above the dreadful difficulties of his past to serve his country throughout his own very distinguished but disability foreshortened 19 year military career in the United States Army . . . and an extraordinarily heroic life—as had his father, Jimmie Hobday.

I heartily recommend reading this story with its incredible "hinges of fate" appearing as mysterious as any fictional novel but validated by numerous revelations of fact . . . and finally, very substantial documentation and heartbreakingly long overdue terminal familial acknowledgement.

Although Dane Hays and I have yet to meet, and as is so often the case, the journey of compatriots, from strangers to friendship, is very short . . . I hope that we have helped Dane to the slightest degree that he has helped ME in knowing of and having a picture of his Dad's crew and reestablishing contact with Fred Parker, completing the "rest of" THIS fascinating and compelling story! I am honored to be considered worthy of writing this difficult Foreword to this story of TWO of our nation's heroes, father, and son, Jimmie Rowland Hobday & Dane Hobday Hays, separated too long by time and distance and fate, but now surely to be bonded in eternity.

Respectfully

Bud Farrell, Author

"NO SWEAT"

CHAPTER ONE

SEDONA, ARIZONA—PRESENT DAY

"You are nothing but a little bastard, and you will always be a failure." Those words had echoed through my head since I was about three years old! Father would say them over & over, never giving a word of encouragement or an even a complement. Then when mother would get into one of her depression or moods and he wasn't around, she would pull out a faded little photo and say in a hushed voice, "If he hadn't been killed in the war he would be your daddy." Then she would speak his name softly, glancing around as though she did not want anyone to hear her say the name.

The first time I ran away from home was at six years old. We were living on my grandparent's farm. Mother had been in a bad mood all day. She had given me several severe whippings which I felt were not deserved! That night she stood at the door screaming and begging me to come back to the house. It so was dark! I was afraid of the dark! Pulling my little red wagon all piled with clothes and toys, I planned to walk up the dirt road to my grandmother's house in the dark. I was only six years old so I turned back because

1

I was scared of the dark. When father got home, he kicked me like a football across the living room floor and then gave me another whipping.

Because of that night, father became forever more frightening than the dark! You remember things like that all of your life! On that fearful night I became a chronic runaway over the next ten years. That night also started a lifetime of physical & emotional abuse from both parents, which took several years of counseling later in life to resolve. Father had said so often that I would be a failure that I eventually believed him. My self-image was zero from an early age!

The best thing he ever did for me was to kick me out of the house at age sixteen just after I graduated from high school. Physically looking older, quite often resulted in people treating me more like an adult when we first met. However, that usually changed after they had a chance to know me. Fortunately older looks did help me survive a rough time in my life! Usually I was hampered by my youth and lack of simple work and social experience.

Tried to go to college, even worked part time for a while and took just a few classes, but I was too emotionally immature and couldn't relate to the people around me or the real world. It was difficult to accept the possibility of success in life because father had beaten into me the notion that I would be a failure. Enrolling in the community theatre program in Phoenix and taking acting classes, helped create a facade to cover failures and inadequacies. Slowly I learned how to get along with other people, grudgingly accepting the fact that success was possible if you really tried! I could have been a success in acting or several other professions if I had known more about real life and been more mature emotionally.

However, several jobs were obtained during those early years by lying about my age and faking entries on a resume until the employers discovered the deception and fired me. Occasionally an employer would offer to keep me on despite the lies on the job application and I have often wondered what my life would have been like if I had taken them up on their offers. Without fail, every time an employer reached out to help me I ran away from the situation.

Spending time, as a hippie in the 1960's in Hollywood was exciting and tragic too. Of course, trying drugs, a commune and group sex was part of the game. Begging for handouts on Hollywood Boulevard or sitting on Santa Monica Pier, smoking joints and trying to "feel" the ocean waves. I could never really seem to fit in with the crowd no matter where I was or what I was doing. When I looked in the mirror it felt like I was "outside" of life looking in.

Working part time as an actor in Phoenix and then going back to Hollywood for a while provided good and bad experiences. For a couple of months there was a good job with ABC Studios in Hollywood and the New Steve Allen Show until they too discovered the job application had fake information. Taking acting classes in Phoenix and studying theatre at Glendale Community College also brought me into contact with another young man & budding actor who would be destined for fame, Nick Nolte.

Nick was a student at Glendale College in addition to both of us working with Actor's Inner Circle Repertory under the Direction of Mel Weiser & Kit Carson. My favorite play was the production of "Royal Hunt of The Sun" where I worked on the stage sets & lighting. Nick was great in his role. Everyone felt that he was going to be someone special. However, I had the most fun with a Children's Theatre production of "Poor Dad, Mama's Hung You In The Closet and I'm Feeling So Sad." The reviews said that I played a "lively corpse." Using a stage name was the rage then, so each time my name appeared in print I changed the spelling. Quite often I used Dayne Hays and eventually settled on my real name to keep it simple.

In time, the training and skills from work in the theatre began to help me overcome my social & work inadequacies, especially while I was still under legal age. Early teen years were spent observing the behavior of important people, trying to find a 'successful' pattern for myself. At first, because of youth, when applying for jobs where

I pretended to be older, hours would be spent reading aloud from the collected works of the philosopher Emmanuel Kant. As a result, my voice would take on a more "cultured" resonance which helped to create a "persona" for that particular job. The downside of that practice was that I couldn't always keep my stories straight and sometimes people would see through my lies.

By the age of twenty-one, I had had so many varied jobs and experiences that creating a false image was no longer necessary. Shifting focus again, time was spent observing personalities and behaviors of influential people that I met. Often adopting what I had perceived as the best of their traits. Sometimes that worked and other times it caused more problems, but I kept on trying. I desperately wanted friends but did not know how to be a friend!

Meeting the manufacturing tycoon, Edgar F. Kaiser Sr. in 1962 during the second year of high school proved to be a learning experience. Mother was working part time in a toy store and allowed me to come in after school to sweep the floor and run errands. Mr. Kaiser wore white linen suits, spoke in a very soft voice, and had several assistants that did everything for him. When Mr. Kaiser went into a store he would indicate an item he wanted to buy with the nod of his head, the assistants would make the arrangements but he would never actually touch the item or speak directly to the salesperson. Mr. Kaiser was cold, very impersonal in his manner yet he gave off the impression of always being in charge. Trying to copy that behavior for a while was difficult and it just wasn't right for me. A lesson learned!

Then in 1968, as I was trying to leave the hippie life, I began working in the basement mail center of the ten-story Tidewater Oil Building at the corner of Wilshire Boulevard & Crenshaw in Los Angeles. The job was to sort incoming mail and distribute it to the various offices in the building. One elevator was off limits except when the others were unavailable. The oil tycoon J. Paul Getty had offices on the 10th floor and it was his private elevator. We received all sorts of instructions about how to act, speak only when spoken to and how to respond if we ever ran into him. A couple of times I had the pleasure of meeting Mr. Getty while on my delivery rounds and found him to be the very opposite of what I had been told. If we were alone, Mr. Getty was always very polite and friendly. He usually initiated the conversation as we rode the elevator or passed in the hallway. If other folks were around, he was the stuffy and gruff person they had described. Mr. Getty always remembered your name and never talked down to you. That was impressive! I liked him!

While playing at being a hippie in Hollywood, a lot of time was spent at Griffith Park wandering through the trees and daydreaming. On weekends, there was always a 'love-in' with music, mood dancing, free food, and of course marijuana. A favorite music group was a young trio that sang together and played the guitar, asking for nothing but a donation dropped into an old coffee can. I would sit on the lawn, eat a sandwich and listen to them sing. Sometimes that was the only meal for the day. Later the singing trio became world famous as the singers Peter, Paul & Mary. Despite intentions to live a 'free & happy lifestyle', in time I eventually became a real 'messed up' person in the head. Don't get things wrong, there were many good times during that part of my young life. Some of them I remember with a smile. However, mistakes, immaturity, and poor judgment often overshadowed the best times making life difficult.

In truth, the hippie life of the 1960s was not so great for most of us! Money was always short, sometimes food too. Some folks would be downright rude to you just because of the way you dressed or asked for a handout. On occasion after partying for several days, you would wake up one morning to find everyone gone along with all of your meager belongings. Certain folks took the philosophy of "community sharing" to the extreme which often made me very uncomfortable! Life began to spiral out of control once again. After spending a few days in Los Angeles County Hospital because of a drug overdose, I returned to Phoenix, Arizona to start over again. Childhood fantasy had turned into a cruel reality.

Down at the bottom of the pit and nowhere to turn! Friends in Arizona had turned their backs on me because of my lies &

carefree lifestyle. Family members did not want me around, and some prospective employers shook their heads as they saw through my attempted deceptions because I was underage, immature, and inexperienced. Life was miserable! Several times I had been close to considering suicide and had half-heartedly attempted it a couple of times. My parents offered no support, advice, guidance, or simple love.

Then one day a newspaper advertisement for a job caught my attention. It was at Turf Paradise horse race track just outside the Phoenix city limits, cleaning the dirty stalls. The job could possibly be the way to clean up myself mentally and start rebuilding an emaciated body with the hard work and long hours. Was I even capable of doing that kind of work? Other than being a warm body, I had no job qualifications whatsoever for the position. I was a pitiful sight! Pale, five foot six inches tall and weighing barely 105 pounds.

Billy Jacot was a former jockey and a horse trainer that ran a small stable of mediocre racehorses. Trainers were required by Federal law to have new employees fingerprinted and a criminal records check had to be completed before they could start to work. Fortunately, all of my legal troubles had been while I was underage. There were no serious offenses but the thought of a police check still caused worry. Looking back at the situation Jacot just needed a warm body for cleaning stalls and I was perfect for the job!

A week later, still groggy from lack of sleep I reported to work at 4:30a.m. The end of every day was pure agony for the first couple of weeks. Slowly my undernourished and drug weakened body responded, gaining confidence & physical strength with each week. When the season ended at Turf Paradise, many of us laborers migrated to Ruidoso Downs in New Mexico or Hollywood Park in California, taking jobs with several different stables. The work was not glamorous but at least it was a job. I could at least pay my own rent; buy food, clothes and maintain a worn out Volkswagen Bug.

One of the trainers I met at Turf Paradise, John Dillard, was a highly respected Owner/Trainer from Texas. John bred quality thoroughbreds as a hobby and hoped that his daughter would carry on the tradition when she got older. His stable was located across from Billy Jacot's and he would often visit with us when he was not busy. John said he would start my training on the horses as an exercise boy, if I went to Ruidoso Downs when the season ended in Phoenix. Since he paid more than Billy Jacot did, I packed up a borrowed 16 foot travel trailer and headed for New Mexico. I rotated stables several times over the next two years trying to find one with better pay and a good trainer, always looking for something different and never finding it.

Only to realize later that John Dillard was an honest & fair man and a good owner/trainer. Two of the best people I worked for were Herb Jolly and John Dillard as they treated their employees with respect, giving a fair wage too. Sometimes a part time job would come up like washing dishes at local roadside diners, providing some extra spending money. Then a short season at Hollywood Park and eventually back to Turf Paradise. Moving up to the job of exercise boy was a challenge, it was better hours but still very hard work. Jolly & Dillard were hard taskmasters. Despite my hard headed attitude they did teach me a lot. Working with the horses and learning things from the two trainers provided a new outlook on life. Then there was the offer from John Dillard to make me an apprentice jockey if I stayed with him and signed a contract. Mr. Dillard had an easy going yet firm manner. He taught me a lot about horses and I learned a few things about myself too. Sometimes I "over thought" a situation which usually resulted in bad decisions, so I quit the Dillard Stables twice, thinking I was going into a better job.

Later I would realize how good the position with Dillard Stables had been and then I would go back to him asking for another chance. Luckily, John hired me back each time! Even though I never won or placed in a race, each one was a small victory for me physically and mentally. Loving the horses, but not liking the idea of working six or seven days a week, twelve to fourteen hours a day finally brought a day of decision. After almost three years of shoveling manure and exercising horses, I decided it was time to make a change, return to Phoenix, and find a new occupation when the racing season ended.

After two months of lounging in the sun, chance provided a job as a clubhouse & swimming pool attendant at a condominium complex run by Hallcraft Homes in downtown Phoenix near Encanto Park. After working ten months for Hallcraft, enough money was saved up to begin part time classes at Glendale Community College. Later, selling vacuum cleaners & swimming pool chemicals and driving a taxi on the night shift for the Phoenix area provided a minimal income. My savings began to grow, and then come close to zero because of my partying habits. In between jobs & love affairs for a year or two, attending college classes, sometimes working as a janitor at night and barely passing the classes in the daytime if I could stay awake. Life was good, so I thought!

For some reason I kept sabotaging myself every time someone gave me a chance! It seemed that as I reached the one-year mark in a job something inside of me forced me to leave. Eventually, I landed a job at Sky Harbor airport in Phoenix, as the dispatcher for the airfreight company, Air Support Systems. The job seemed to have potential for the future, providing I could keep myself out of trouble because I was still trying to party every night.

During the two years as dispatcher with the airfreight company, I met some interesting people and learned a lot more about myself too. However, one person made a lasting impression in the way I perceived people of influence. The restaurant in the main air terminal at Phoenix Sky Harbor Airport had a corner section of the lunch counter that was reserved for airport employees. Sometimes, high profile folks that were waiting on their planes would eat their meals or have a cup of coffee at the counter to avoid contact with the public. The airport employees always gave the VIPs a respectful amount of space and never spoke to them unless they spoke first. Employees were supposed to just blend into with the woodwork!

One man was definitely the exception! He would always take the time to chat with us while traveling from his ranch near Tucson back to California or another destination. The actor John Wayne, trying to avoid attention, would walk into the airport terminal wearing dirty Levis, soiled shirts & muddy boots that quite often had dried horseshit on them. John would carry an old feed sack over his shoulder and often sported several days' growth of beard. Surprisingly most people never looked at him twice or recognized him! When John sat down at the lunch counter with us he would look at our nametags, always calling us by our first names and asking us to call him by his first name also. John would continue sitting and talking with us as long as no one asked him for an autograph or talked about his movies. John Wayne would talk about any subject except acting. If someone did come up asking for an autograph, John would politely excuse himself and quickly leave. John was always friendly no matter what your job, making every day small talk as though he had known you all of his life. John Wayne's way of dealing with people was an important lesson for me about treating everyone as an equal.

For a while, the airport dispatch job was successful until I ended up partying too much and mixing with the wrong crowd again. This time, I did get smart and walked away from the people and places that were a bad influence on me. Because of poor planning and over confidence, I had failed to find a job before I quit the freight company so it was a shock when job interviews kept turning me down. I had overpriced myself, still lacking the proper job skills & experience for most of the positions that I wanted or felt that I deserved. Debts were piling up and a live-in girlfriend that spent all of my money just compounded the problem. I needed a job fast!

One day at the Christown shopping mall in west Phoenix, while putting in job applications, I passed by an Army Recruiting Office with a poster in the window asking "What Can We Do For You." Walking into the office on a lark, I handed my neatly typed three page job resume to a Recruiter, SSG Williams. Telling him I would be back in an hour to see what he could offer me. In reality, the military as a job was the furthest thing from my mind yet the benefits listed on a wall chart in his office were very appealing. I needed to pay bills plus I was in a bad relationship and this could be a way to solve the problems.

Returning an hour later from another failed interview I wasn't so cocky! SSG Williams had already scheduled me for the written test and physical exam for the next day at 6am. A whole day was spent being tested, poked, prodded, and interviewed. Fortunately I passed everything. The enlistment counselor offered several jobs that were not related to combat and kept coming up with additional incentives to entice me into signing. I finally gave in and enlisted in the Army as a Personnel Clerk that afternoon, and boarded a plane for Basic Training three days later on the 14th of February!

I still remember Drill Sergeant Pick's laugh at the Fort Leonard Wood Reception Station when I told him I joined the Army for one hitch just to pay off some bills. SSG Pick already had me pegged. I was going to be a 'lifer'! Basic Training at Fort Leonard Wood wasn't easy, especially since it was the worst winter Missouri had had in decades.

We lived in an old World War II 50-man Quonset hut, double-bunks set six feet apart. I had the top bunk with a florescent light fixture hanging down just three feet above me. I couldn't sit up in bed without bumping my head on the metal frame of the light. There was a small oil heater at one end of the room and the metal walls of the Quonset hut had a gap of two inches between them and the cement floor. Our latrine/showers were in another Quonset hut about 50 yards away with lots of mud in between. At least they had a narrow cement walkway between the buildings! It was cold, wet, smelly, just plain miserable!

As the training progressed, physical, and mental well-being improved and I found that the discipline & regimentation of the military life actually suited me. Basic Training still sucked! I understood the need for discipline and quick reaction but hated every moment of the stress, constant harassment by the Drill Instructors and of course the physical exertion. The combat & physical training was difficult as I had never been very athletic and I knew nothing about handling weapons. The Drill Instructors would sometimes fudge my firing range results because they were losing too many people. Unfortunately, some things never leave you, no matter how hard you try. I could not seem to forget how father was always calling me a bastard and saying that I would always be a failure in life. Would this enlistment in the army end in failure too?

Fortune smiled once more! After Basic at Fort Leonard Wood, advanced schooling (AIT) was at Fort Ord California, near the beautiful towns of Monterey & Pebble Beach, for training as a Personnel Records Specialist. The Instructor, SGT Alvarez, was taking night classes at the local college and luckily most of them were courses I had already taken. Seeing an opportunity, I offered to help him on his homework in exchange for less work details. SGT Alvarez readily accepted the offer, as his grades for those classes were low.

His assignments required me to spend a few hours in the public library each weekend but that was a small price to pay to have free weekends for the next two months. Once his homework was done I would take advantage of local activities. Taking the two-dollar bus ride into Carmel to the USO Club for the free lunch every Sunday was the perfect escape from the barracks and surprise work details. The USO also offered a free bus tour of the Carmel/Monterey area after the lunch which finished up just in time to catch the last transit bus back to the base.

Enroute to my first duty station after graduation from AIT, I took two weeks leave and returned to Phoenix. Seven months in the Army had done wonders for me and I felt like a stranger visiting my old haunts. After three days of partying I was ready for a change, that old way of life was not so exciting anymore! Full of confidence and a new level of respect for myself, as I snapped to attention before my new commander, CPT Williams as I reported in to my first duty assignment as the only Personnel Records Clerk at Yuma Proving Grounds in Arizona. Realizing years later that this was one of the best assignments of my entire career!

The first Officer I worked for at Yuma was Chief Warrant 4 Cantrell. The Chief sensed there were some buried problems and became a mentor, guiding me towards a successful career and pounding some common sense into my thick head. Cantrell allowed me use of his car so I could drive into town to take night classes at the local community college. Only two classes were needed to complete the two-year degree from Glendale Community College outside Phoenix. The Chief constantly encouraged and helped me to pick up additional military skills by requiring me to take correspondence courses and attend additional schooling. In some ways, Chief Cantrell was like the dad I never had!

Leaving Yuma a year later fully qualified in two more military career fields and authorized to be an instructor in the new field of data conversion & computer programming. From then on, I strove to be an over-achiever to make up for my past failures and quickly became a "super trooper," receiving early promotions and many awards. I had found a lifetime occupation in which I excelled and didn't have to create an image or hide behind a mask. Ironically, all those years of doing just that had provided the skills to succeed in some very strange and varied assignments during the course of my military career.

There was still that empty feeling inside, because the "family" just didn't want me around despite my attempts to improve myself. Father had said that there was no room in the family cemetery because I was a 'bastard'. Not really a part of the family! Trying a few more times to reconnect with my parents, each meeting ended with indifference and failure soon convincing me it was a waste of time. On military insurance documents, my parents were listed as whereabouts unknown and a friend was named as insurance beneficiary.

Due to job requirements working as a Nuclear Surety Specialist, I received a higher security clearance than most soldiers and began to expand my duties & training with each new assignment. Over time, I performed duties as a quality assurance specialist, instructor, S-1 NCOIC, Battalion Personnel Senior Staff Advisor, JAG Inspector,

Intel Specialist, and several other positions. Advanced promotions and continued schooling over the years eventually boosted me into an elite category within the worldwide army structure.

As a teenager, both grandmothers had given shelter and support over the years, even sent money when they could save up a few dollars and had often defended me against snide comments from some members of the family. Because of the constant running away from home both sets of grandparents had said if I could make it back to North Carolina they would let me live there and be safe. Mother's words about that man being my father "if he had not died in the war," and the man who I thought was my father always calling me a "bastard," kept haunting my life.

I tried so hard to bury those thoughts and feelings, without success! There had always been unexplained bits and pieces of memories floating around in my head from early childhood. A warm voice, a smile, a youthful face, playing in a bare yard in a place I did not really remember. Those pictures and sounds were always there in my dreams, haunting me throughout my life. Where did they come from? Who was that person with the voice that felt so comforting? Why did my father hate me so much?

CHAPTER TWO

AM I GOING TO DIE?

Now at sixty-one years of age and feeling like a hundred years old, disabled from military injuries and living in a nursing home because I cannot take care of myself on the outside. The Veteran's Administration Doctor had given a diagnosis of a terminal condition with maybe six months to live. When he said to quickly put my personal affairs in order, I thought all hope was lost! It was impossible not to think about the past in that situation. You find yourself contemplating your life, pondering the 'what ifs' and wondering what you could have done differently.

Looking at all the 8x10 pictures I had put on the wall showing all the things I had done in my past life. Trying to brighten up the hospital like room, yet unable to mask the odor of the soiled linen cart parked in the hallway by my door, or the moans from the ninety-year old Mrs. Anderson in the room next door. Was this going to be my fate until I too slipped into that mental fog of oblivion? Would I become like many of the other residents in this nursing home, unable to care for myself or even know what was going on around me? The future did indeed look bleak.

At least for now I could keep my Medical Alert Service Dog in the private room with me. Buzz was a highly trained and intelligent Border Collie & Australian Shepard mix. That dog knew hand & voice signals and understood conversational English better than some people that I knew. We had been through a lot over the last nine years and I felt lost without that dog. He could sense my need for pain medication or when I was about to have a seizure or debilitating muscle spasms in the legs. A generous friend had obtained Buzz from a local organization and had the dog school trained to assist me as well as to be my companion. I needed to be alerted on the seizures and the need for medications and Buzz kept me in his sight all of the time. By the time Buzz was six years old he had surpassed all expectations in his abilities and his devotion.

After three heart attacks, the doctors felt a second angioplasty was needed, despite the diagnosis of a "terminal" condition. A second angioplasty produced limited improvement. Doctor Frank Nagy was one of the staff doctors at the nursing home and a retired Army physician. Though it was frowned on by some of the staff he would often befriend patients that were veterans and take them on short excursions. When he was introduced to me, all he saw was a frail man in a wheelchair that could barely move and function. Doctor Nagy felt compassion for this old & frail veteran and took me to lunch at a local restaurant one day. It felt so invigorating to be back in the real world! I didn't realize it at the time, but the more Dr. Nagy talked with me, he began to suspect that the VA's terminal diagnosis was wrong.

Dr. Nagy took me on a motorcycle trip a few weeks later as a sneaky way to confirm his suspicions. He arranged to have two other veterans go with us; one of the men was a nurse. One would ride his motorcycle and the nurse drove his VW Bug carrying Buzz in the passenger seat. As I rode on the back of Frank's motorcycle I could see Buzz watching me intently with his head hanging out the window of the Volkswagen. We headed for a nearby lake, barely an hours ride though it felt like an eternity.

Eating lunch in a rustic café by the lake and returning to the nursing home mid-afternoon. Frank had loaned me a helmet which was too big for me as it kept sliding forward covering my eyes. The bouncing, oversized helmet did not matter. I was having too much fun! The bike ride was invigorating! Feeling the fresh air rushing past and even riding through a light sprinkle of rain, just made me feel alive once more. Later, as I was looking at the photograph Frank took of us sitting outside the restaurant, it gave me quite a shock. I had not realized that all of my hair had turned white.

Eventually Doctor Nagy began to firmly believe that the VA's diagnosis was incorrect. That I was either not terminal or didn't have Parkinson's disease. He decided to test his theory by offering to take me and Buzz on a three day camping trip to Lake Powell a month later. Dr. Nagy would take photos of my activities and keep a detailed journal of what he observed. The nursing home had not wanted me to leave the property so both of us had to sign several liability waivers before I was allowed to leave the facility. Despite the fact that Doctor Frank Nagy was on their Board of Directors!

The heavy metal folding wheelchair took up a lot of space in the small seventeen foot aluminum boat. Feeling and looking like a hundred years old, the trip was a challenge physically and emotionally draining for me. I was worn out before we even arrived at the lake after the five hour drive! Thankfully, the doctor had extra camping gear and clothes that fit me. My strength was so poor that he had to push me in the wheelchair everywhere. I tried to get around with my cane but could only take small steps and after a few feet I would be out of breath, suffering extreme pain.

It was great to be outside! Fresh air, peaceful and quiet! I could only walk a few feet without resting and each step sent spasms of pain up through my feet and legs. I was even too weak to lift an overnight bag without effort. I don't know how I survived that weekend! I struggled through each day, just trying to do little everyday chores. The scenery was beautiful, the open air invigorating, yet there were several moments when I regretted agreeing to the adventure. Persistent weakness, pain, and shortness of breath plagued me the entire trip.

Buzz worked constantly, keeping an eye on me at all times. Never allowing me to be out of his sight for a moment yet still trying to be a dog on a new adventure. Buzz would tug at my pant leg when I needed to rest or rest his paw on my arm when I needed to take pain medication. At night he slept beside me in the tent Frank had set up, always keeping some part of his body touching mine. Boating was a new experience for him and that dog just took it in stride as if he had been doing it all of his life! No matter what we did, Buzz stayed focused on me day & night, always alert to warn me of a problem. I tried to walk around the campsite and help, sadly discovering that I was so weak, even the simplest activity left me breathless.

Returning to the nursing home late Sunday afternoon we were met by overly concerned medical staff, anxiously awaiting our return. It took four days to recover from that trip and yet I hungered for another chance to go again. Despite the negative attitude from some of the staff members of the nursing home! I think the photograph Frank took upon our return speaks for itself. I was tired but felt empowered and alive for the first time in over a year!

Frank Nagy sat down with me a few days later to explain what he had observed, showing me some of the photographs that he had taken of my activities. He was firmly convinced that I had been misdiagnosed and there had been no further decline since my arrival! Since Frank was not my primary-care doctor or associated with the Veteran's Administration he was treading on dangerous ethical territory. I agreed to let him use his staff physician's status at the nursing home to run some tests and attempt to modify the medications that were prescribed. If his theory was correct we could then present the results to my Veteran's Administration doctors and request them to re-evaluate my medical condition & diagnosis. It would require me to keep detailed, sometimes hourly notes as to what I was feeling and how the medications affected my body. Having worked in medical administration many years earlier that training would prove useful once again.

After several months of difficult testing and medication changes, his written report was given to the local VA outpatient clinic which they in turn forwarded to the regional VA Hospital in Prescott. A few weeks later the VA changed their 'terminal diagnoses' and ordered additional tests to verify Doctor Nagy's theories! Some of the new medications that he had prescribed were already providing pain relief and I was visibly regaining strength. Would I have a second chance in life? Possibly leaving the nursing home in the future?

Four months earlier the VA Cardiac clinic at the Prescott VA Hospital had certified my heart was "perfectly okay", despite the fact I had already suffered three or more heart attacks in just a couple of years and had one angioplasty. New cardiac tests were ordered, this time at an independent facility. Thanks to a doctor at the Arizona Heart Institute, further testing indicated a 70% blockage in the heart. The blockage was discovered within the first hour of four hours of testing! The VA was notified and they approved emergency surgery at the Heart Institute to remove the severe blockage.

Returning to the Sedona nursing home a few days later after surgery, I was still weak and confined to the electric wheelchair but we continued testing out new medications. This time the testing was done with the full consent of the VA outpatient doctor. Different combinations of medications were tried with varying dosages, refining the results and maintaining meticulous notes. Finally Doctor Nagy felt he had the right combination but one final step had to be taken to prove his theory. A "medicine holiday," where you reduce down the prescribed amounts until you either are at zero or back to the original conditions. As in my case, such a practice can be painful and potentially deadly. Within two weeks I was back to the identical condition in which I had arrived one year earlier.

Recovery was slow as the medicines were restarted and slowly increased. However, Doctor Frank Nagy's theories were proven undeniably correct! I was not dying! The new medications did make a difference once the heart problem had been corrected. Eventually I received a letter from the Veteran's Administration Hospital stating that my terminal diagnosis "may have been wrong" and they would have to do additional tests. I know other veterans have faced similar situations and this proves once more that sometimes a second or third medical opinion can be a life saver for anyone. Just because one doctor makes a declaration, does not always mean it is correct! It didn't seem possible that I could ever be able to live by myself again. Or how much longer I would live with all of the various medical problems that were occurring. The future still looked grim! Yet there was hope!

CHAPTER THREE

Mother, long suffering from mental illness and finally diagnosed later in mid-life with schizophrenia, and tormented by her hidden past continued to slowly decline mentally and physically. She had been in so many mental hospitals since 1949 I had lost count. She was currently residing in a small nursing home outside Phoenix. After father died, she continued to live with her relatives in North Carolina. Eventually family members gave up trying to take care of her and asked me to assist despite her objections, so we moved her to Arizona.

Once again she was changing nursing homes, as the present facility could no longer take care of her needs. She was being transferred to a larger nursing home north of Phoenix in a couple of weeks. One of the Sedona nursing aids was hired to drive me down to Phoenix on his day off in his truck. The plan was to go through all of her stuff hoping to find a few items to sell and weed out some of the junk that she had collected over the years. Maybe I would be lucky, making enough money to pay off some of her bills.

What we found instead was sad and disappointing! Most of her stuff was now trash, or she had torn it up during her temper tantrums. Three years earlier, I had moved her from North Carolina to northern Arizona into a very nice nursing home up in the pine tree country of Flagstaff. We had combined furniture as she had left most of her stuff in storage in North Carolina. I had even given her some of my antique furniture that had been kept in storage for several years against the day I would need to settle down permanently. My antiques matched most of her furniture too. Shortly after settling in, mother began giving away many of the expensive pieces of furniture to complete strangers, including my contributions.

After several emergency room visits, I became suspicious. Searching her rooms we discovered two suitcases full of old prescription bottles. Most of the medications belonged to other people and some were actually harmful to her. Mother was self-prescribing and taking various doses of the pills just because she thought she knew better than the doctors did! Sadly the nursing home staff had not done a thorough search of her belongings when she first arrived. Because we took away her medications and placed restrictions on her, mother became irate, returning to some of her old habits. She convinced a couple of nursing home housekeepers to help her sneak out of the facility and move into a rental home in the west side of Flagstaff.

Then mother fell victim to some people that stole most of her good furnishings and a lot of her money. Since she had been convinced by them that I was "out to get her money" mother refused to talk to me. There was no way I could help her until Adult Protective Services (APS) finally stepped in and took over her care. Responding to a phone call from a passing utilities repair crew, APS had found her living in a double-wide mobile home that had no electricity. She was hungry, dirty, needing medical care and the new mobile home had been trashed inside with most of her belongings gone. Her dog was starving and had left deposits of urine & feces all over the house. Over the next year APS had to transfer mother to three different nursing homes as she was always complaining of abuse, theft or something. Only later was it discovered that all of her allegations were figments of her imagination. Sadly her complaints had caused some workers to be unjustly terminated from their jobs.

Now I had to move her again. This time moving her would not be so easy! The few pieces of furniture that remained were of little value. Close inspection revealed the stuff was in such bad shape three used furniture stores and even the Salvation Army refused to accept the remaining items. However, mother had managed to have additional boxes, previously in storage in North Carolina, shipped to her. Those boxes had to be sorted, and the unusable items disposed of before she could be moved. We had to promise mother that her belongings were going with her to the new nursing home. In reality, she was about to be transferred into a hospital type room that was very small and she only have but one or two small items.

The Phoenix nursing home director kept mother busy out on the patio while we sifted through boxes of clutter. Some had been in storage for a long time or stacked to the ceiling in her bedroom closets. This time I was making sure there was nothing of value or any contraband hidden in the room before the movers arrived. Mother had a habit of hiding things in the strangest places. When mother had first moved from North Carolina we had found a loaded rifle & two pistols that she had somehow smuggled into the nursing home from her old house. We never could figure out how she had managed to bring them in unless someone helped her. While going through her clothing it wasn't unusual to find left over food stuffed into the pockets or unopened mail tucked in strange places.

Mother had been a yard sale junkie for years. Habitually hoarding useless items that she would never use but firmly believing she needed them. There were several boxes of women's high heel shoes, fancy dresses, & coats. Most of them still had thrift store price tags still attached and were not even her size. Mother adamantly held onto those boxes, yet she would quickly give away priceless antiques because they did not match her décor in the house or as payment for someone going to the grocery store to buy her milk! While at the nursing home in Flagstaff, I realized one day as I was putting away her groceries that she had over twenty glass measuring cups. Asking if she would give me just one cup was a big mistake! She became very angry, started cussing, and told me to leave. If you tried to remove a single item from the house mother would throw a temper tantrum and she always had multiple reasons for her hoarding.

Both closets in that Phoenix nursing home room were stacked with her boxes and there were more boxes placed under and around her bed, leaving just enough room to walk. Why had that been permitted? Mother even had additional boxes in the storage room of the facility. Many of them contained old magazines & newspapers she had collected over the years just because she liked some of the pictures. Sifting through one of those boxes, I noticed a tattered manila folder stuck inside a magazine. Inside the folder was a large well-worn brown envelope. There were several packets of letters and photos with three smaller brown envelopes inside. Most of the items were from her boyfriends that she had during World War II and afterwards.

I knew about many of those boyfriends and some of the affairs both my parents had kept up, even after they were married. In later years, both would claim they had been virgins & high school sweethearts, always true to each other. I knew different! When they had arguments the names of each of their affairs would be yelled back and forth. Mother would say she dated the men before marriage, yet some of the dates scrawled on the back of the pictures were after her marriage! I had even met some of the men she "dated" when I was very little. For many years during my childhood, she had kept a large photo album on a shelf that she would show me when father was not around and tell me about the people in the pictures. Eventually the albums fell apart and she stuffed the photographs into a shoe box.

When my parents drank and partied, their personalities changed! Usually, they would not associate with any of the neighbors but were always available to party with anyone from the commercial aviation industry. The airlines would have regional or station parties, usually at some fancy resort which they loved to attend. Sometimes I would spend the whole night in the back seat of the car while they partied. Most of the time they would leave me home alone for the weekend or with strangers and go party. Bringing home lots of pictures back, telling stories about how much fun they had on the trip or at the party. Then asking me if I had been okay with all of the frozen TV dinners' they had left for me in the fridge. They were always bringing home lots of souvenirs from the trips, but not one of them was for me!

Looking through this collection of pictures and letters was bringing back many old memories from the past. Opening a slightly smaller faded brown envelope, the snapshots inside gave me a real shakeup! Instead of more boyfriend pictures', there was something different inside. Unexpected! An 8x10 glossy photo of a B-29 bomber flight crew posing in front of their plane was on top. Three photos of a young man, two of them in his teen years, possibly school pictures. Obviously, he had a big growth spurt at the end of high school. Very clean looking and quite mature for his age in one photo. A familiar look in his eyes and smile caught my attention. Did I know him? There was something about his face! Several photos from the 1940s of people, mostly couples and I did not recognize any of the names.

Inspecting the pictures once more, that feeling came over me again. It was as if I had seen the young man before, but stronger. Could I have possibly known him when I was a small child? Strangely, the pictures gave off a warm, comfortable, and safe feeling. Quite the opposite of when I looked at any photos of the man that I had known as 'father'. Why was mother saving these pictures, keeping them separate from her other snapshots? Why were they so important to her? How did mother manage to keep these hidden for over sixty years? Who was this young man? What was her connection to him? Why did he seem so familiar to me?

The larger of the photographs, an 8x10, I guessed was a Korean War era B-29 Flight School Graduation photo, probably taken at Randolph Air Force Base in San Antonio, Texas. Despite many years of storage, it was in excellent shape though quite brittle. Many years ago, a couple of the boyfriend photos had been in the albums that I had looked at as a child. This collection with the air force pictures & letters I had never seen before. Still remembering those times as a youngster when mother would be in one of her depression moods, how reverently she would pull out the photo albums and look at the pictures. Mother would still sift through the pictures periodically, even after she had crammed all of them into a couple of shoeboxes. These were different. She was giving them a special status for some reason. Why were these so important?

As I continued to look at that flight line photo, something inside of me jumped & twisted! It was such a strange haunting feeling that I set the prints down and took a deep breath before looking at them again. Mother's voice echoed in the hallway. She was still outside on the patio talking about someone she had met years ago. I could hear her complaining, as she wanted to come back inside the house. Mother did not like to be out of her room for very long, it was her sanctuary. I realized that despite the cool air conditioning I had started to sweat. Time was short and I needed to make some quick decisions about her personal items and decide what I wanted to take with me before mother came back inside.

I could not pull myself away from the photos without great effort. Hurriedly, I looked through the contents of that manila folder again before we boxed up a few items for me to take back to the nursing home in Sedona. On the flipside of the air force photo was a list of all the crewmembers and their jobs and present ranks. A notation penned in one corner and signed "Love Jim." Who was Jim? Why had she kept these items hidden and separate from the rest of her stuff? Why did this man's face give me such a strange feeling?

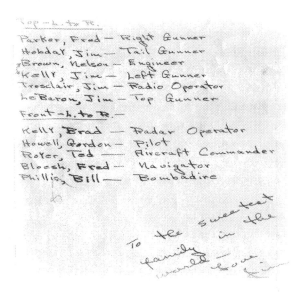

Top – L. to R.

Parker, Fred – Right Gunner
Hobday, Jim – Tail Gunner
Brown, Nelson – Engineer
Kelly, Jim – Left Gunner
Tresclair, Jim – Radio Operator
LeBaron, Jim – Top Gunner

Front – L. to R. –

Kelly, Brad – Radar Operator
Howell, Gordon – Pilot
Roter, Ted – Aircraft Commander
Blocch, Fred – Navigator
Phillips, Bill – Bombadire

To the sweetest
family in the
world love Jim

One of the names unexpectedly caught my attention and then it hit like a bolt of lightning! Jimmie Hobday! Suddenly I was transported to my early childhood days when mother would finger that well smudged picture. Jimmie Hobday was the same name my mother used to say, whenever father was not within hearing. That man "would have been your father if he hadn't been killed in the war"! A name that had haunted me throughout my life! The same name was on the back of the Air Force photo as a 'Tail Gunner'. How had mother managed to keep this envelope and its contents hidden? Images and voices from my childhood long forgotten, suddenly burst into shape and crystal clarity! Childhood dreams were becoming reality and my gut was doing flip-flops! My heart was pounding as mother's voice ricocheted in the hallway. She was coming back inside the house!

Quickly, with trembling hands, I stuffed the collection back into the large envelope, gently placing everything inside a cardboard box that was already overflowing. Wiping the sweat from my forehead and trying to regain composure as they walked into the room. While we kept mother occupied the aid quietly took the boxes outside to his truck. The nursing home director explained to mother once more that she was going to be moving to a new room and that movers would pick up her belongings after she had gone ahead to her new home.

The hour and a half drive back to the Sedona nursing home room felt like an eternity! Watching the freeway mileage signs slowly go by, all I could think about was that cardboard box and the manila folder with those pictures and letters. I hoped that mother would not miss that envelope or look for it anytime soon! I did feel guilty for taking it without telling her. Yet, in her current mental state she probably will never miss it. The trip felt like time without end as I pondered the name of Jimmie Hobday and the long forgotten images from my childhood. Jimmie Hobday's name, my childhood memories and the contents of that packet just kept leading to more unanswered questions and bewildering emotions.

Upon returning to the overcrowded Sedona nursing home late that afternoon, I began to unpack the boxes and sort the contents. Finally finding courage after dinner to reopen the large brown envelope and examine the contents in detail once more. Jimmie Hobday must have been very special to mother. She had saved several letters from him in addition to all of the photographs. There were several with a Cortez postmark in addition to those with a military postal stamp. Some of the letters were intimate in nature, often asking about 'the baby'. Sometimes even mentioning my name! What was so special about Jimmie Hobday? What was his connection to me and to her? There had to be a way to find out more about him! Bravely, I placed a phone call to my mother's younger sister Sarah in North Carolina, casually dropping Jimmie Hobday's name during the conversation. Aunt Sarah gave such a strong reaction and negative response that I dropped the subject quickly! Her parting comment had been "Why do you want to know about that boy? He was nothing to your mother!"

The military had taught me how to go through various resources to find out information, utilizing the various government databases. That knowledge would prove to be very useful in my research. Luckily there was unlimited internet access right in my room. I started the hunt for B-29 Tail# 44-86343 and Airman First Class Jimmie Hobday. A name that had haunted me all of my life! His young face, etched into memory since I was a small child! As days passed by new memories kept popping up from my early childhood. Now I had letters and photos of him, only older, but still with that same great big smile and those dark gentle eyes.

Days and weeks flashed by as though time was standing still! I neglected Buzz at times and began skipping some of the "social activities" designed to get the residents out of their rooms. Consumed to the point of obsession, by a desire that I couldn't understand or even comprehend I spent hours on the computer. Staying up late, often working only by the light of a small lamp on the computer desk. Up early every morning checking for email replies before breakfast and then back at the computer throughout the day. Spending every waking moment on the computer searching all of the veteran's groups and any information related to B-29s in Korea. Looking for any scrap of information on Jimmie Hobday. Searching for answers to questions I dared not voice yet they rolled around in my head with ever increasing pressure. My heart pounding with excitement at each new discovery!

Comparing the dates I realized that all of the letters and pictures had dates matching the time when we lived in Cortez, Colorado or later in Prescott, Arizona. Calling the Cortez school district and the public library provided the first clues. There was a young man by that name who had attended Montezuma-Cortez High School during that same period in the late 1940s. The school district located some old microfiche records on Jimmie Hobday and after a little convincing, they mailed me a copy. Receiving those records a few days later provided enough information, with a little creativity, to request his birth certificate and military records from the Military Records Storage Center in St. Louis, Missouri. I began to build a chart and time line that matched Jimmie's life in Cortez and the military with that of my own childhood. This was no longer just a coincidence! Too many things were falling into place! Could we be related?

Posting notices with over a dozen veteran's organizations that had websites, repeatedly sending inquiries to military reunion groups. Spending countless blurry-eyed hours combing through military archives and numerous government historical records with only a little success, I was very thankful for a private room! The nursing staff left me to take care of myself most of the time as long as I made it to the dining room for meals and a few of their planned activities. I appeared to be medically stable and sound of mind. That left the staff free to handle the more difficult residents during the work day.

Hours were spent searching for any scrap of information or other clues, usually without solid results. Two folding TV trays, set by the desk, were stacked with manila folders & papers. Notes pasted on the wall by the desk, reminders on websites or inquiries. Then I began an exhausting search of the Hobday name in the regional phone book indexes, sending out inquiries asking if they were of any relation to Jimmie or his family. Within days, replies started coming back from folks, all saying that they were not related. Still no word from the various veterans' groups, yet there was always hope something would turn up.

Two weeks later an email from Jim Boardman, the Base Historian at Randolph Air Force Base in San Antonio, Texas was received. Randolph Field had been where much of the initial B-29 flight training had occurred during the Korean War. There was a photo of Randolph Field in the packet mother had, along with several notes & souvenirs from the San Antonio area. However, I knew that my parents had never been to San Antonio so it just left more unanswered questions, more mysteries, and more frustration!

Jim Boardman had said he would forward a free copy of a book on the B-29 training during World War II & the Korean War. The book was a Department of Defense publication with a chronological history of the Air Force training programs. Included would be some reference material that might help in the search for answers. According to Jim, there was more information on the private veterans' group internet websites than in the available official military records. He suggested several websites to check out, all of them new to me, except for one that I was already using.

There was also a sketchy listing in the Korean War Memorial database in Washington D.C. The website not only indicated soldiers that had died or listed as Missing in Action but provided some family information and the awards earned by each soldier. Typing in what little information I had on Jimmie, it provided me with a few additional clues. The narrative stated how Jimmie had died and all of the medals awarded to him. However, there was no photo of Jimmie or of any family listed in the database, just the notation "No known next of kin."

A few days later, retired Air Force NCO Ed Moynagh sent me an email. Ed was involved in searching for missing families, trying to match DNA of unclaimed bodies and those soldiers listed as Missing in Action from the Korean War with possible surviving family members. Apparently remains of soldiers from the war were still being found and returned to the United States by North Korea. I had replied to an inquiry Ed had posted on one of the military websites. He was offering to assist anyone looking for information of missing people from the Korean War. Just on the chance that it might help with my own research I felt it was worth the try. Surprisingly, Ed actually had A1C Jimmie Hobday listed in his working file!

He was able to provide additional material and more referrals to several military websites. I explained my own quest and a possible relationship to Jimmie Hobday, providing him with information I had gathered from mother's batch of pictures & letters. Ed felt that I had enough documentation to pursue a formal investigation and provided me with contacts at the Pentagon. Finally finding the courage to voice a question I had been avoiding, he agreed that Jimmie & I might be related. His guidance enabled me to expand research into more productive areas and each day brought new hope with more information. All Ed Moynagh asked in return was the chance to clear up Jimmie's case file.

AMERICAN BATTLE MONUMENTS COMMISSION

 The Korean War Honor Roll

Jimmie Rowland Hobday

Cortez, Colorado

Born May 26, 1932

Airman First Class, U.S. Air Force
Service Number AF17329984
Missing in Action - Presumed Dead
Died September 13, 1952 in Korea

Airman First Class Hobday was a crew member of a B-29A Superfortress Bomber with the 371st Bomber Squadron, 307th Bomber Wing based at Kadena Air Base, Okinawa. On September 13, 1952, while making a bomb run on the Suiho Hydroelectric Plant, his aircraft was hit by anti-aircraft fire. He was listed as Missing in Action and was presumed dead on February 28, 1954. Airman First Class Hobday was awarded the Air Medal, the Purple Heart, the Korean Service Medal, the United Nations Service Medal, the National Defense Service Medal, the Korean Presidential Unit Citation and the Republic of Korea War Service Medal.

KORWALD Loss Incident Summary

Date of Loss:	520913
Tail Number:	44-86343
Aircraft Type:	B-29A
Wing or Group:	307th Bmb Wg
Squadron:	371st Bmb Sq
Circumstances of Loss:	Hit by AAA and exploded in mid-air over Suiho Hydroelectric Plant

Crewmembers Associated With This Loss				
Name (Last, First Middle)	Rank	Service	Status	Comments
BLOESCH, Fred E.	1LT	USAF	MIA	
BROWN, Nelson M.	MSGT	USAF	MIA	
HOBDAY, Jimmie R.	A1C	USAF	MIA	
KELLY, Henry B.	1LT	USAF	MIA	
KELLY, James W.	A1C	USAF	MIA	
LE BARON, James R.	A1C	USAF	MIA	
LOWE, JR., James A.	CAPT	USAF	MIA	
PARKER, JR., Fred NMI	A1C	USAF	RMC	RMC Big Switch
PETERS, Spiro J.	1LT	USAF	MIA	
PHILLIS, William K.	1LT	USAF	MIA	
ROYER, Ted G.	1LT	USAF	MIA	
TROSCLAIR, James O.	A1C	USAF	MIA	

Jimmie Hobday was no longer a ghost! He was a real person. I realized finding information on him would be difficult because so many years had passed since his death. After all, the Air Force had not been able to locate very much information on Jimmie in the last fifty years! Jimmie Hobday died young and tragically. His high school Junior Yearbook had a definite anti-war comment under his name. There too, lay a mystery, why he had changed his mind after high school about the military and joined the Air Force.

Perhaps it was the situation with my mother, or it could have been when he received word about one of his friends, Johnny Spruell, who had quit high school & enlisted in the Army? Johnny had died on 6 December 1950 in Korea, just before Jimmie enlisted in the Air Force. So many questions, so many different paths leading into a puzzling maze.

Then Jimmie Hobday's military records arrived in the mail. It took a few days to cross reference the information with what I had already discovered. The records now provided a more thorough picture of his life. By comparing several of the letters and photos from mother's packet to the Air Force Records and the other items I had received, many details of my early life and Jimmie's were matching up. Conversely, every scrap of new data always seemed to lead to more unanswered questions.

The Cortez city librarian, Beth Harper, who had previously provided assistance, had gone to high school with both men. Beth had told me a lot about Jimmie & John and the Cortez neighborhood in which they had grown up. Both boys had lived only a couple of blocks apart and had been close friends. We had lived only two blocks away from both men during the same period!

Jimmie apparently had a difficult time when Johnny quit school and joined the Army. Beth knew that Jimmie's older brother Richard had died sometime in the 1950s but was not sure about his sister Joan who had dropped out of sight also in the early 1950s. Was Jimmie really my birth father? He was so young! The boy was still in high school when I was born! Would mother have married him instead of the man I knew as my father? Is that why father always called me "a bastard"?

Comparing the few photos of myself, from when I was about the same age as those that were in mother's packet, and from Jimmie's high school yearbook provided a few small clues. Many similarities and differences too! Everyone said we did look alike, especially when we were younger. He was taller than I was as an adult, yet both of us had undergone fast growth spurts, going from childish faces to mature men very quickly.

According to the school & birth records, Jimmie only had the older brother Richard and his sister Joan. There was only one grainy photo of Richard in the high school yearbook a couple of years before Jimmie graduated. I finally located one yearbook picture of Joan but it was so poor that even the computer Photoshop could not clear it up. Continuing to compare photographs, and constantly asking others to compare them too, some folks said I looked more like his older brother Richard in the face and I had to agree. More unanswered questions!

Why had Jimmie Hobday listed mother for notification in case of death with the Air Force, but not his parents or siblings? I still remembered the day mother received the letter from the Air Force when I was very young. We were living in Prescott, Arizona at the time. Where were his parents? Did they have any more children besides Jimmie, Richard, & Joan? Was anyone in that family still alive? Had mother planned to marry him? Did other family members know about the situation around my birth? If he was my birth father why was his name not on the birth certificate? A thousand questions and no solid answers! It was just a waiting game until someone answered one of the many internet inquiries. Perhaps I would luck onto something in my research.

The best chance was a reply to the many requests that had been made through various active duty military channels and the military retiree websites. There were several email replies from military bases, saying that they were not involved in the B-29 training or that they were not open at the time. Some bases had changed names after the war, or closed and reopened years later making research difficult. Finally the point was reached where nothing more could be done! I had to wait until someone replied or forwarded additional information. Perhaps, I would be lucky and stumble upon something that might provide some further clues or information from some of the Korean War books that I had recently ordered.

The internet search consumed every bit of free time for weeks. I stayed up late on the computer, hurrying through meals or required social times. Getting up early in the morning and going back to the computer, constantly looking for replies to any of my inquiries. Hours spent searching for more websites and databases, delving into the government archives for scraps of information. Meanwhile I was keeping in touch with Ed and the contacts at the Pentagon, keeping them updated as to my findings. I felt consumed with the overwhelming need for answers!

Repeatedly leaving messages with all of the military reunion groups and service organizations, I was always hoping for a positive reply. Then contacting military bases again, this time asking for access to their libraries and the various official government information agencies. Slowly the realization hit! This search had started years too late! It was almost 58 years since the war ended. Most of the people that would have known Jimmie were probably dead or too old to be involved. Many government records had been archived and were no longer readily available online. Emotions began to weigh me down, feelings of defeat and despair. Failure!

Here Buzz & I were, marooned in that nursing home! The youngest person there and most of the residents were either too senile or too ill to carry on a meaningful conversation. No living family members that cared or that I would even consider asking them questions about Jimmie Hobday & mother. The phone call to Aunt

Sarah had produced such a reaction I did not feel safe in bringing up the subject of Jimmie again. There was no town which to call home. There was no one alive that I could call 'real family' as I had spent my life knowing or feeling I was a "bastard child" and the family that raised me did not want to claim me as one of their own.

Most of my childhood years were spent being shuffled between foster care, various family members, and sometimes strangers because my mother was always "sick." The Army had in fact, become my surrogate family! I was lost without the military, the discipline, the control, the purpose in life! Now I was stuck in a nursing home with the doctor's decree of a terminal illness which would slowly destroy my brain and then my body. After all, I was supposed to be dead in six months! Perhaps the additional testing scheduled for next month would show something different. As the result of their earlier diagnosis, I had given up all of my belongings and continued to suffer ever-increasing pain day & night, despite the heavy medications. You had to wonder how and if the Veteran's Administration could ever make up for my loss or the problems their terminal diagnosis had created. What was my future? How long did I have to live? How soon would my mind cease to function?

Injured in the Line of Duty in 1990, the service injuries had kept me in Fort Hood Military Hospital for ten months leaving half my body not functioning correctly. Unable to walk and having considerable difficulty talking or even functioning normally on a daily basis made life very difficult. A lot of hard work and a slow healing body had at least provided a chance to have some semblance a life again for the last ten years. Unable to handle a manual wheelchair, the VA had eventually issued an electric mobility chair which was a lifesaver for me.

Fortunately, ten years after I was injured I could finally walk with the aid of a cane and live an almost normal life though I still required a large amount of medication on a daily basis. Buying a 38 foot customized motor home, I had become a full-time RVer traveling most of the year. Then three heart attacks in one year, right after a VA doctor had said that my heart was "perfectly sound." That was not enough! It seemed like my body was rebelling with new problems constantly appearing. No matter how hard I tried to compensate or what the doctors did, things kept getting worse.

Suddenly I was going downhill physically and medically. My legs had quit working again, and I could barely stand, then with a wide variety of other unexplainable symptoms with excruciating pains. Life was becoming miserable once again! The VA doctors at the outpatient clinic in Lake Havasu city had conducted a multitude of tests, forwarding the results to the regional VA Hospital in Prescott. After several additional tests and more questions the Prescott doctors sent a final report back to the Lake Havasu Clinic.

Upon review, the Prescott VA had decided upon a terminal diagnosis of a very progressive form of Parkinson's disease. A few days later a Social Worker came to visit my home in Lake Havasu for two hours. Her written report was added to the previous reports. After the doctor's had reviewed all of the results their decision caused the Veteran's Administration to place me in the nursing home on two-week notice. Unfortunately, you cannot take a VA doctor to court for mistakes or problems caused by their diagnosis or treatment!

The home in Lake Havasu with the landscaped yard & swimming pool was gone! The 38 foot customized motor coach that I had traveled from Mexico to Alaska in, gone! A lifetime collection of memorabilia from around the world, gone! Rare books & coins, artwork, even the military uniforms all gone! Fortunately I was able to donate many items to three different museums and spent several afternoons packing & mailing off large boxes. All of my worldly possessions were now reduced to what would fit into this nursing home room. There had been barely enough time to scan two footlockers of documents & photographs onto CDs before the contents were shipped off to the museums. At least I still had a computer and my dog!

Information on Jimmie Hobday's past was slowly starting to fall into place, there was no doubt now as to my relationship. He was my birth father! I was excited yet sometimes I felt like a trespasser, delving into the personal history of families and people from the past. Communicating with people I didn't know and did not feel comfortable in telling them that I might be Jimmie's son, or at least connected somehow. Most folks in Jimmie's generation were not computer buffs so I was surprised to learn several of Jimmie's high school friends were on the internet. Chuck Haley was one of them and he had known both Jimmie & John Spruell. He said that many of the classmates still lived in Cortez.

Then Chuck sent an email with unbelievably great news! Jimmie's sister Joan, who had entered a Convent in 1952, was still alive and living just under two hundred miles south of me in Tucson. Chuck even had an address so I could write her a letter! Joan had attended their 50th high school reunion a few years earlier in Cortez. That afternoon I sent off a simple hello letter without revealing anything other than I was a retired veteran assisting in locating families of military members listed as Missing in Action. Having never spoken with a Nun, I was unsure of conversation dos & don'ts and taboo subjects. Would Joan even talk to me? What did she know about Jimmie's past? Did she know anything about me? About mother?

As more information became available through the research, I kept Ed Moynagh updated so that he could eventually close the file on Jimmie. With Ed's help, I was able to copy the flight school photos and submit them for a records correction to the Air Force and the American Battle Monuments Commission. Jimmie Hobday was becoming a real person, no longer listed in the government database as an unknown without a photo or background information. It would help if the Air Force could contact his sister, as they wanted to talk to her about a few things. Even without her, the Air Force could now close his file and give him an honorable burial.

The Air Force Casualty Branch at the Pentagon assigned Mr. J.B. Wiles to keep in contact with me after I finally told them I thought I might be Jimmie's son born out of wedlock. Sending them

Jimmie Rowland Hobday

Cortez, CO
Born May 26, 1932

U.S. Air Force
Airman First Class
Serial Number AF17329984

Missing in Action -
Presumed Dead
September 13, 1952

Airman First Class Hobday was the tail gunner of a B-29A Superfortress Bomber with the 371st Bomber Squadron, 307th Bomber Wing based at Kadena Air Base, Okinawa. On September 13, 1952, while making a bomb run on the Suiho Hydroelectric Plant, his aircraft was hit by anti-aircraft fire. He was listed as Missing in Action and was presumed dead on February 28, 1954. His remains were not recovered. His name is inscribed on the Courts of the Missing at the Honolulu Memorial.
Airman First Class Hobday was awarded the Air Medal, the Purple Heart, the Korean Service Medal, the United Nations Service Medal, the National Defense Service Medal, the Korean Presidential Unit Citation and the Republic of Korea War Service Medal.

THE KOREAN WAR VETERANS HONOR ROLL

copies of letters, photos, and the information I had gathered during my research, they agreed. Several of their staff commented to me that it was a common situation and that it would be treated as a confidential matter. The Casualty Branch staff would work with me and together we might find some answers to all of my questions. Within a couple of weeks an updated copy of the American Battle Monuments Commission listing for Jimmie Hobday was received. It had his photo from the flight school picture alongside the narrative.

CHAPTER FOUR

-SISTER MARY JOSE (JOAN) HOBDAY-

Having discovered Jimmie's older sister Joan, a Nun since 1950, was alive and living nearby I was apprehensive and excited. I wanted to have as much information ready as possible before talking to her, so I discussed the situation with J.B. Wiles at the Pentagon Casualty Branch. He said Joan needed to talk with them directly and that she may be eligible for several things if she was interested. Calling the phone number that Chuck Haley had given me and having to leave a message left me a bit anxious.

The next day Sister Mary Jose (Joan) Hobday returned the call. Not knowing just what or how much Joan knew I was very cautious in what was said over the telephone. After all, she was a Nun! Carefully explaining to her that I was retired from the army and assisting in searching for the families of soldiers listed as Missing in Action with no next of kin. I told Joan that we had just corrected Jimmie's records and since she had been located, the Air Force Casualty Office needed some information from her.

We talked for almost two hours. Joan was in poor health but at least I could talk with her! Joan, Sister Jose as she preferred to be called, emphasized that when she entered the Convent she had "shelved away" emotions & memories from her past. She did not like to relive those old memories. The Air Force had actually notified Joan of Jimmie's death during the war and she had refused to become involved any further at that point! As we talked, Joan (Sister Jose) eventually accepted the fact that since Jimmie's records had been corrected she did need to discuss things with the Air Force.

However, Joan was adamant that because of her age, illnesses and most of all her religious training, the combination prevented her from "digging up the past & letting loose the ghosts" as she described it. Sister Jose was almost blind, having to use a bulky magnifying machine to allow her to read so usually a volunteer acted as her private secretary reading aloud her correspondence. The loss of vision was due to problems from Diabetes, and she was fighting cancer and several other medical problems. Sister Jose did promise that she would call the Air Force Casualty Branch tomorrow morning.

Sister Jose and I had two more long telephone chats that week. I wrote her a long letter telling her a few more things about myself. We began trading phone calls and letters on a regular basis, each time both of us cautiously revealing more about our own lives. A letter arrived from her written on the Fourth of July 2008. We had previously discussed my parents living in Cortez and some of my life achievements. Joan did not remember ever meeting my parents but felt that Jimmie might have met them after she left Cortez. Sister Jose promised to continue to follow up with the Air Force and thanked me for taking interest in her brother.

Sister Jose continued to trade letters with me every other week, usually discussing an item from our previous phone conversations and always slipping in something new about my past. She would also ask some blunt questions about my life, which I tried to answer honestly and diplomatically. In turn, Sister Jose sent several thought provoking letters that she dictated to her assistant. I obtained several of the books & taped lectures from an internet bookstore that Sister Jose had published so that I could understand more about her. Sister Jose had an excellent public speaking voice and was witty yet very frank and direct. Even on the most serious or controversial topics!

Because of my mother's mental problems and her fascination with Christian Science I had become somewhat agnostic in my religious beliefs. However, as one gets older and wiser we tend to change our outlook on life. I had attended several different mainline churches as an adult and felt stifled or put off by rhetoric and overbearing personalities, eventually finding a balance with a few small independent non-denominational churches. Periodically I donated my off-duty hours to the churches and had even worked as lay staff for a couple of them. Sister Jose found several of my comments amusing as we discussed some of my observations. One of her favorite sayings was "Faith takes many forms."

As time went on, the topic of conversation would always turn to Jimmie when we talked on the phone. The Air Force Casualty Office would also call Sister Jose or send her letters. She would then call me, read the letter aloud, and ask what they wanted or what a particular action would accomplish. Sister Jose changed her mind several times, regarding what she would allow at the Cortez cemetery or even to what she desired from the Air Force Casualty Division. At one point, due to doctor's orders Sister Jose stopped all actions and contact as she was on strict bed rest at the directive of her Catholic doctor. She said that she had to divest herself of all responsibility and "return to basic Catholic philosophy."

When Joan became a Nun, she "buried" mentally & spiritually, all of her past, her family, everything! As a result, receiving all of the various communications and requests from the Air Force in addition to being in contact with former friends from Cortez, and an "old lonely Veteran" like myself eventually became too much for her to handle. It finally became clear that at Sister Jose's age, with her training and background, she was either unable or unwilling to deal with all of these "buried" memories. At times she spoke as though these things were happening to someone else and she was just an observer. This left me frustrated at times!

The Air Force eventually sent Sister Jose a package containing corrected copies of Jimmie's military files and included a small wooden display box with all of his military medals. She sent her usual short note on the 9th of November 2008:

"Dear Dane . . . Peace and good be to you. Here's the letter I mentioned. Its' just an overview! The medals arrived. It is difficult for me to look at them, Dane. Such small substitutes for a life, yes? I'll be praying for you especially on Veteran's Day. I wish you every blessing . . . . Love, Sister Mary Jose."

Despite severe medical problems, some with terminal consequences, Sister Jose was always upbeat and cheerful on the telephone or in her letters. Her attitude in real life was a mirror image of her lectures and books. Sister Jose was always very upbeat, positive and thought provoking. She kept informed on the latest trends, social controversies, and political activities around the world. Just the opposite of what I had expected from a Nun! I was fascinated by her intellect and wide variety of interests.

Sometimes during our early conversations, she would let slip a perceptive comment, letting me know that she deduced more than I realized about my past. Within a couple of months, we found ourselves making small talk on the telephone and Sister Jose was constantly sending little notes & cards each week in the mail. Sister Jose (Joan) Hobday had become a close friend in a short time. It was easy to forget that we had never specifically discussed my possible relationship to her and Jimmie.

When Sister Jose had medical problems she endured the time quietly and did not write or call until she felt better. Then she would call me with that exuberant voice, often wanting to discuss some item of note from the local or international news. I was constantly amazed at the depth of her knowledge & understanding of current national and international affairs. While talking with her on some social issues it was so easy to forget that she was a Nun. Sister Jose was well educated and took an interest in many social & political areas. Nothing seemed to be off limits in her discussions, yet I was still hesitant to bring up my own situation and our relationship. I wanted to do it in person, not by telephone or letter. This occasion needed to be special and personal!

CHAPTER FIVE

CORTEZ, COLORADO—SIXTY-TWO YEARS EARLIER

Jimmie Hobday was on his way home from school. He had been playing ball with friends, and was going to be late for dinner. Hoping that his sister Joan would not fuss at him too much for getting his slacks dirty as it was only Tuesday! Then he noticed this very shapely young woman, in the front yard of a small, shabby slate-sided house, just a few blocks from his home. Many of the houses in this area had been built by the same company and were almost identical in appearance. The woman was at least 19 or maybe older with lots of freckles and long bright red hair. The yard was bare except for a couple of patches of grass. There was a gravel driveway on one side of the house with a wire fence separating it from a trucking company next door. A thin cement sidewalk lead up to the front door stoop. Despite a fresh coat of white paint the screen door hung precariously looking like it would fall off at any moment.

She was sitting on the porch steps. Her bright auburn hair, hanging down below her shoulders, shimmering in the sunlight. Jimmie's friends constantly kidded him a lot because he looked so young and was bashful towards the girls at school. It is just the way he was on some things! Jimmie couldn't resist the temptation to stare a bit, she was pretty, and she noticed him looking too. "Hi, my friends call me Mott, would you like something cool to drink?" Jimmie went up the narrow cement sidewalk towards the front door where she was standing, holding the screen door open. Knowing he would be late for dinner, Jimmie still followed her inside the house. He was nervous yet drawn to Mott for some unexplainable reason.

Over the next few weeks, Jimmie dropped by several times on his way home from school to visit Mott for a few minutes. Usually he spent the afternoons at one of his friend's houses or at the school, so his sister didn't worry about him or ask questions. Mott was always dressed in something very thin and tight. It was still warm outside at this time of the year, but her clothes were rather provocative even for that time of the year. It was difficult not to notice! Jimmie felt a bit embarrassed for staring at her. But she was pretty!

Mott's husband, John, worked at the small municipal airport for Monarch Airlines that had just started service at Cortez with DC-3s. John always came home late and you could hear him a block away as he rode an old military-issue motorcycle. It was very noisy! Mott was lonely, and liked to talk. Jimmie could spend all day talking with her while she told him stories about growing up in North Carolina or some of the places they had lived.

Sometimes Mott would put a record on the phonograph, or tune in some music on the radio. The two of them would dance for a couple of songs. Mott had offered to teach him to dance so he could ask a girlfriend to one of the school dances. Mott was a good dancer and always held him close, much nicer than the girls at school. Jimmie was still a bit shy on some things. Mott's dancing made him feel more grownup. At the same time made him feel a bit strange. Jimmie was very self-conscious about the fact he still looked very boyish and that his voice had not evened out yet. Mott was an older woman, five years older than his sister!

Jimmie didn't plan to stay very long, but somehow the visits kept stretching out. Mott always had some lemonade or had a soft drink for him. Sometimes she even had homemade fudge or a piece of cake. Then, Mott started giving Jimmie a kiss on the cheek as he would be about to go out the door. Soon that little kiss turned into a real kiss and her dancing became more touching than dancing. At first Mott's closeness and touching upset Jimmie then he began to like it even though he had never done things like that before. Mott was always so friendly. She talked to him like an adult despite his youthful appearance and age.

Jimmie was confused and torn between emotions and his family teachings. He was a good Catholic! Mott was married! You did not "get involved" with married women. Jimmie's parents had taught him respect and honor. This situation just kept getting him more mixed up inside! Especially, since Jimmie was about to turn sixteen and definitely underage, and still looked even younger. He liked her attention yet it scared him too!

Jimmie's older brother Richard had already left home to work for the government, and his big sister Joan was talking about becoming a Nun after college. His mother died last year, only a year after his dad had died. Jimmie's sister, Joan, was taking care of him and trying to keep him out of trouble. Joan felt he could handle things his last year of high school on his own and so she was going to be leaving for college next year.

Jimmie had always had such a baby face until his junior year of school was almost over. Then he started having a growth spurt. Recently everyone begun to remark that he was starting to look older and quite often acted a lot more mature than many of his classmates. There were not too many girls at the high school that interested him. Sometimes his shyness prevented him from becoming friendly with the girls in his classes. Mott's attention made him feel more grownup nonetheless it was very unsettling.

Mott was very appealing. Their afternoons became more frequent and she was definitely suggesting that she wanted to take him to bed. Jimmie was still a virgin! What was he supposed to do? Things were getting complicated at home too. His sister Joan was trying to make ends meet, and planning for her move to the college at the end of the summer. Joan was still talking about joining a Convent later on, or some other type of service to the Church. She would let him spend time with his friends from school as long as his schoolwork was finished before bedtime. Never saying a word about him spending the time with them, when he could be doing chores at home or even when he was late for dinner. She was a very understanding and forgiving person! Their mother had raised them that way and this thing with Mott really complicated the whole situation. Jimmie did not like hiding or lying about how he was spending his time after school.

Jimmie spent many nights agonizing over the whole mess that he had unintentionally gotten himself involved in! He should go to Confession or at least talk to a Priest, but he was afraid of what might happen. Would this cause more harm than good to both of them? Jimmie's Church teachings made him realize that he was in big trouble spiritually and legally too. He was thinking constantly about the lessons on "Mortal Sin"! Life had suddenly become very complicated!

A couple of weeks went by very fast. As Jimmie was walking down the street on the way home from school one afternoon, he hesitated, saying to himself: "What am I doing? I want to go all the way. Some of my friends have already done it, but I'm afraid." Jimmie did not stop walking, he just went at a slower pace, trying hard not to look at the house down the street. Glancing up he saw Mott. She was waiting at the door as usual, dressed in a very light, almost see through dress that had a flowered print and was very low cut in the front. Even though he didn't want to, Jimmie still turned and went up the narrow sidewalk towards her door. Today for some reason, there were beads of sweat on his forehead. As he came up the walkway, Mott smiled and opened the door for him to come into the house. The top two buttons on her blouse were unfastened. Her smile urged him to quickly step inside the house.

Joan was beginning to worry about Jimmie. She had not mentioned anything to him but it was all too obvious that something serious was bothering Jimmie. He had been skipping some of the activities at the Church and even missing evening Mass, which he had never done before. She was sure Jimmie's homework assignments were not up to his usual level of thoroughness. He hadn't mentioned his grades or homework lately or even asked for her advice and that caused her concern too. Jimmie had always asked for her advice or guidance, especially after mom had died. Whatever the problem it was causing quite a distraction.

Most striking was Jimmie's lack of spontaneous laughter and big smiles. Something was wrong and it was apparent that Jimmie didn't want to talk about it! If Jimmie did not snap out of it soon she was going to have to intervene, possibly making some decisions that he might not like. Joan was still responsible for Jimmie even if he did feel that he could handle things by himself. Their mother had always stressed open communications & honesty between family members, along with the delegation of responsibility. Joan had to get Jimmie back on track before she went off to college. Even if it meant that she had to act like a parent instead of a sister/best friend! They had never had a serious disagreement, especially since their mother died, but she foresaw problems if Jimmie did not make some changes soon. Perhaps she needed to seek guidance and pray on the matter.

INTERLUDE

World War II was over. Soldiers were returning from the war and trying to pick up the pieces of their former lives. Finding jobs, or trying to fit in with families that had grown and changed. Some wives had found 'boyfriends' while their husbands were away at war and wanted a divorce. Many families, especially the wives, could not handle the mentally and physically wounded men that returned from the war. Men needing reassurance, validation they were still 'men' inside, despite the loss of an arm or leg. Kids were afraid to hug dad at bedtime because he had a hook instead of a hand or was missing a leg. Men wanted to leave the small towns and seek new jobs or lives in the larger cities.

America was a country that had to rebuild itself mentally, and spiritually, changing the way it had done things just a few years earlier. Rethinking their values and way of life as it had been in the past. Young men in high school felt anger & frustration. School children were learning about the Atomic Bomb. A new fear was slowly creeping into the hearts of the average American citizen. War was a dirty word that brought back terrible nightmares and reminders of hard times. Nobody wanted to go to war again but it was always a constant topic of discussion. No one wanted to have to kill another person or see the horrors that their dads & uncles had seen, but rarely talked about. Yet, at night, you could hear the former soldiers talking in their sleep, waking up yelling, or jumping at loud noises, scaring the family with their nightmares from the war. The way of life for America had changed forever because of the war.

CHAPTER SIX

DANE—THE EARLY YEARS

I can remember very clearly, the first time mother showed me the little photo and said, "He would have been your father, if he had not been killed in the war." She was having one of her moody spells and had been crying for some reason. Mother cried a lot and seemed to be sad all the time. The photo was so worn and smudged I couldn't really see the face in the picture. Mother would often repeat Jimmie's name, as though he was someone special. She would never bring the photo out, or say anything in front of father. In fact, quite often I sensed mother was afraid of him even seeing the picture or hearing Jimmie's name. Father had a temper, he would yell at her or even at me sometimes and I was still too young to understand why.

As time passed and I got older, father's anger and resentment toward me became more obvious. There was always some excuse for him not to attend a school function, or to be involved in some activity with me. My parents argued all of the time, sometimes it felt like they argued about me or that I had caused the argument. Every so often I knew for sure the argument was about me! Mother was sick a lot and he would often blame me for her problems. I was usually sent to live with relatives or strangers when the arguments became real bad or when mother had one of her depression spells. Sometimes mother had to go to the hospital because she was so emotionally out of control. When that would happen father always made me stay with someone else, as he didn't want me in the house.

Once, he tried to teach me how to fish when I was about five years old. The first thing I did was get a fishhook caught in my finger. Grabbing the fishing pole out of my hands he told me to go away and give him some peace. He never even attempted to teach me about fishing again! That was how he treated me for the rest of my life! You could always hear him mutter under his breath. "He is just a bastard, going to be a failure all of his life." How I hated to hear those words, they really made me feel like a piece of dirt! Mother would always act as though she did not hear him say anything and never once spoke up for me!

We did a lot of weekend camping, just so father could "get away from the office." Most of the time when we went out in the desert or up in the mountains dad would just tell me to "go play but don't go too far," and then he would ignore me until they were ready to go home. It was mother's job to see that I was fed and where I slept. Many times it seemed like taking care of the dogs and finding firewood were the only reasons for my presence.

Even though both grandparents had televisions as early as 1952, father finally brought home our first television set when I was in the fourth grade in 1957. It was a used Motorola in a giant wooden cabinet with a very small screen. When I was at someone's home as a young child, and saw programs like "Ozzie & Harriet," "Father Knows Best" or "Leave It To Beaver" I would find myself uncomfortable watching the shows as my childhood reality was so different. Those families could not be real!

Rarely did I have exposure to "healthy" families so there were no good role models for me to follow. Staying with my grandparents in North Carolina was great but sometimes they had problems too.

Yet both sets of grandparents were always kind and loving to me. Most of my aunts & uncles were tolerant and a few were abusive. Occasionally I was allowed to stay with second cousins on the Hardison side of the family. They were always nice people and treated me kindly. Some of the other people I lived with as a small child had just as many issues as my parents, so knowing "proper behavior" and how to act weren't always easy.

We moved around so much while I was in grade school that the only way I knew where we had been was to look at the shoebox full of report cards. I know I went to two different schools for the first grade, three schools for the second grade, and three schools for the fourth grade. I did about half a year each for the first grade, but for the second grade one of them was for only a couple of weeks. I could never catch up on my schoolwork because of the moving around, so I did a lot of reading at home. Reading was the one thing I did well. I was always at least two or three grades ahead of everyone else in my reading ability but behind in everything else.

My parents did buy me an Encyclopedia Britannica British Edition the summer before the third grade. I was constantly reminded that it was expensive and how they could have used the money for other things. When homework required time at the the school library my parents would insist that I stay at home and use the encyclopedia instead. By the 8th grade the encyclopedia was out of date so a lot of the information would be wrong, causing me to get lower grades. Some teachers would even marked down my homework in English classes because I used the "British spelling" of the encyclopedia words. I didn't know there was a difference! When I told my parents they would say the teacher was wrong or that it must have been my fault for "misspelling the word."

Living on remote airports did have certain advantages for a kid. I was able to play in a lot of old airplane wrecks, and see all sorts of new airplanes fly in for refueling. For most of the second grade, we lived in Nevada on a government airfield south of Reno near the town of Minden. Four Air Force men and their wives were living there too. The Air Force was testing captured German Buzz bombs and rockets from the war and trying to build bigger ones.

Bonanza Airlines made one stop a month at Minden. Their DC-3s brought in supplies, mail pouches and occasionally a few government employees. The rest of the time father acted as a weather reporter, ramp/ticket agent and even as a "spotter" for the government's atomic tests on the other side of the mountain range. I didn't know until many years later, both my parents had been sworn to secrecy about what they saw or heard while we lived at the Minden Airport.

Once we even saw the top of a mushroom cloud from the atomic explosions on the other side of the mountains at the Nevada Atomic Test Center. It caused a cloud of radioactive fallout to drop onto the airport as I was in the yard playing. Mother saw the strange cloud when she stepped out of our little trailer, grabbed me and took me inside. Both of us had little ash flakes in our hair. The only thing the Air Force men did was wash everything down with a water hose. Mother made me take a bath then let me go back out to play. All of us got sick for a few days after that.

Father also refueled the government planes and reported the weather observations on a big and very noisy teletype machine that sat in his office. I could spend hours watching the thin metal arms clatter back & forth. I had read the small metal instruction plates that were attached to the faded grey case so many times I had them memorized. I had run the tracks of my electric train set under the back corner of the teletype machine just so I could be close when it started up.

That part of the Nevada desert was loaded with large Jack Rabbits so every few weeks father and the Air Force men would drive up and down on the runway at night killing the rabbits with their guns. I understood that was the only way they could keep the rabbits from causing the airplanes to crash. I still didn't like it! Because I cried so much the first time I went with them, they left me at home by myself on future hunts. I still cried every time they went on a killing spree! Minden airport was a cool place to live because of all the different airplanes but it was so lonely because there were no other kids around! Most of the time I played by myself outside or in the back room of the office.

The famous Howard Hughes parked one of his airplanes at Minden airfield for a couple of months. Unlike the stories you hear now, Howard was really a kind and gentle man. He was always smiling and talking to me as though I was an adult. Howard was extremely energetic, constantly on the go, yet he would take the time to talk and play with a young child like myself. One time Howard stopped father from whipping me when I made too much noise in the office. So I felt safe around him! Sometimes, he would even bring little toy airplanes for me to play with. Howard had many meetings with groups of government people that would come out to the airplane in big sedans. During his meetings I wasn't allowed to play around the airplane. That plane was more like a hotel room inside, so fancy it even had a big bedroom and a shower.

Howard partied a lot too! Howard even took us to dinner one time at a fancy casino in Reno. Like many precocious seven year olds, I asked to say Grace when the food was served. My mother tried to pretend I didn't say anything. Father scowled and told me to stop talking. With a big smile Howard stood up and yelled out "Quiet everyone, the kid has got to say Grace." The entire casino stopped while I said the prayer! After I finished, Howard chuckled and said something like "I didn't know I had such a loud voice." Occasionally he bounced me on his knee, telling me stories about some of his adventures. I liked Howard and really looked forward to his visits.

Howard took me inside the plane a few times, even let me sit in the pilot's seat. I met one of his girlfriends, the actress Ava Gardner. She was a very beautiful lady! They had a cabin up at Lake Tahoe. He brought her to the airport several times. She would give mother & I hugs when she came to visit. Once, after they had spent a weekend of loud partying she gave mother a set of earrings and a scarf. They had spent one of the nights sitting and drinking in his custom DeSoto sedan which was parked near our trailer. Howard even apologized to mother for making too much noise during the night.

One morning Howard and his pilot arrived just as we were finishing breakfast. He told my dad they were leaving but he might be back in a month or two. He came over and gave me a bit hug, telling me to stay out of trouble. I sat on the edge of the runway watching them load up the airplane. Those giant propellers were kicking up a lot of dust as it taxied for takeoff. I never saw Howard again but like all kids do, I bragged about knowing the famous Howard Hughes.

Father kept in touch with Howard Hughes until around 1970 when Hughes was really starting to get sick. He kept a box full of letters and photographs from Howard that was usually stashed in the bedroom closet wherever we lived. I don't know what happened to that box, it just disappeared and they never mentioned it.

Both parents gave me whippings at a moments' notice, usually it was because they were in a bad mood. I learned early in life that it was safer to entertain myself and stay away from them, especially when father first got home from work. Since there were no kids around to play with at most of the places we lived I had to use my imagination a lot to keep myself busy. As I got older, they would insist that I stay in my bedroom instead of playing in the yard or the living room.

Occasionally a few good things did happen! The best times were when I lived with my grandparents in North Carolina. They never gave whippings or sent me to bed without food, except when I was very young and got into trouble. I was even allowed to play with other kids and have friends! It was a completely different world! I had a bedroom with each set of grandparents and I knew that all my treasured possessions would still be there the next time I was sent to live with them.

I will always remember one special trip, when I was being shuttled back and forth to my grandparents because my mother was in & out of the hospital again. Summer was almost over and school was starting in two weeks. I was flying, all alone from North Carolina to Los Angeles. Back then, airline employees and their families could fly free on any airline so it was easy for father to put me on an airplane instead of driving to Carolina. Kids could even visit the cockpit and talk to the pilots during the flight. Usually I had non-stop flights but this trip I had to change planes in Atlanta, Georgia, all by myself. That summer was my tenth birthday.

Because I was a kid traveling by myself, I was required to sit in the First Class section when a seat was available. The plane in Atlanta was one of the big TWA Constellation planes, very fancy inside. My seat was next to this man in a business suit, he seemed to be very important as the flight attendant kept stopping by to see if he needed anything. They were also constantly checking to see if I was "bothering" him. The man would just smile and tell them we were doing fine. He was a very nice man and his first name was Kirk.

It was an overnight flight, non-stop to Los Angeles so we began to talk. Kirk told me that he had a son my age. We shared some of our snacks & meals. When I was tired, Kirk even put a pillow in his lap, letting me stretch out and sleep. I told Kirk about my mother & dad. How they treated me at home and constantly bounced me between family members or others. Sometimes I stayed with strangers and had to share a bed with their kids or even grown men.

Kirk was very sad about that, saying, "Grownups aren't perfect and they can have problems too. Sometimes those problems unintentionally hurt the children. When that happens, you can either let it hurt you inside and be angry, or you can learn to be strong & forgive them." Kirk said the best piece of advice he could give was

"To always follow my heart, and don't ever give up on your dreams. No matter how much someone says that your dreams might be impossible." I told Kirk that he must be a good dad; he just looked at me and smiled.

Then we landed just before dawn at Los Angeles International Airport. It had been raining, there was a cool breeze blowing. Kirk & I walked down the metal rolling stairs and off the plane, hand in hand. There was a big black car waiting for him on one side of the steps, the driver was holding the door, an open umbrella in one hand. Father was also waiting by the stairs. When we got to the end of the steps Kirk turned to me, shaking my hand and said "Dane, don't ever forget what I told you." He got into his car and waved good-by as they drove away. Father took me by my hand, and we started walking across the concourse towards the airport terminal. He then asked me, "Do you know who that was?" I said, "Yes, that was my friend Kirk. We had a great time!" He said, "That was the actor Kirk Douglas, the guy you liked in that movie The Vikings."

I just could not believe that was Kirk Douglas, one of my favorite actors and I hadn't even recognized him! He didn't look as tall as he did in the movies! I always remembered what Kirk said. "Don't ever give up on your dreams." Sometimes those words kept me going through some rough times! I wanted to thank him in person someday but never had the chance. Years later, after reading his autobiography, "The Ragman's Son," I wrote a letter to his family telling them about my experience but never received a reply. Sadly, the son Kirk had that was my age, died about the same time as when we had been in the plane together.

I finished the last half of the second grade in Reno, Nevada. We had only lived there a short time before mother went into the hospital again. I don't know what happened but I spent a couple of months in State Foster Care while she was in the Reno hospital. I stayed at a "boy's ranch" and it was great! Then mother got out of the hospital and we moved to the little mountain town of Floreston on the California side of Lake Tahoe.

Father commuted to work at the Reno airport in his new VW bug. It was a long drive down the mountain from Lake Tahoe so he would stay in Reno for several days before coming home. I liked it in Floreston because there were other kids to play with, but mother kept telling me the kids were "too rough." Soon she found excuses for me not to play with them. One of the neighbors was a Den Mother for the Cub Scouts. Around the third meeting I caught a cold from one of the kids so I wasn't allowed to go to another meeting. When school started, the parents had to drive the younger kids down the hill and over a small wooden bridge that straddled the Truckee River. Then we would wait for the school bus by the side of the highway. It was a twenty-mile ride up the canyon to the school. I only went to five weeks of school for the third grade in Truckee.

The third grade teacher, Miss Booth, was a tall skinny woman. She wore those real tiny eye glasses that perched on the edge of her nose. Miss Booth was very strict; she would hit your hand with a ruler for the least little thing! She said that moving around, missing school was just an excuse, and that I had poor grades because I was lazy. I got sick at school one day and threw up in the hallway. Miss Booth would not let me leave because she thought I was misbehaving, and punished me by making me stay after school to write an apology on the blackboard. That meant the only school bus going down the canyon would leave without me. I really did feel sick!

The Principal, Mr. Johnson, was closing up the building when he saw me sitting in the classroom crying. "I apologize for being lazy and not doing my homework" was written on the blackboard one hundred times. He had to take me home as everyone else had left for the day, including Miss Booth. Mr. Johnson was upset over the teacher making me miss the bus and leaving me by myself. It was snowing very hard and his small car had a rough time on that mountain road. I was very sick and Mr. Johnson had to stop on the side of the road because I threw up twice. Once he almost did not stop in time, his car would have been a mess.

It was the mumps & measles at the same time! The bedroom at the back of the house was too drafty and cold so I had to sleep on a mattress in the living room near the furnace. A blizzard hit that same week, causing the Truckee River to freeze over. When I got over that illness, something else made me sick too. I was sick for a very long time, even went to the hospital in Reno for a while. The school finally sent some folks to talk with my parents. Later a grade card came in the mail promoting me to the fourth grade without ever going back to school to finish the third grade.

Then we moved another three or four times as dad had new assignments, opening up new airports and training the people. Back to Reno once more for a month, then three different houses in the suburbs around Los Angeles, California. One of them was a big fancy two-story house painted bright pink in Manhattan Beach, #312 Strand Blvd. I could play in the sand or go swimming because it was on the hillside overlooking the water. That place was lots of fun until mother started having problems again! She started seeing 'faith healers', trying to solve her emotional problems. I think father went along with it just to keep her happy!

We became friends with the woman living in the house behind us. Her name was Barbie Whitmore. She worked for Hughes Aircraft Company on the assembly line. When Barbie was much younger, she had been a Hollywood starlet for one of the studios and had been a double for young Elizabeth Taylor in one movie. Barbie had even worked a short time as a private secretary for Howard Hughes. Barbie liked me and told me she was going to be my 'Auntie Mame'. True to her word, Barbie kept track of me until she died thirty years later. Always sending little gifts in the mail or calling to see if I was okay, never asking for anything in return. We would talk about things on the phone that I could not talk about with my parents. Five years prior to her death she moved to Phoenix and my parents took care of her. My parents waited six months before they told me of her death, supposedly I was to inherit a few things from her but the only thing I received was an empty old steamer trunk.

In 1957, father's job with Bonanza Airlines transferred him to the Phoenix, Arizona airport as the Station Manager. We lived on the Pima Indian Reservation south of Phoenix in an old house for the whole school year while I was in the fifth grade at Laveen Elementary School. He had to haul water for us to drink on his way home from work each day. I could play all day in the surrounding desert or visit the Indian families down the road and play with their kids. Mother didn't like me being out of her sight or with other kids so most of the time I had to stay around our house or on the hillside where she could see me.

My fifth grade teacher was Mr. Leatherman. He had been a Captain in the army prior to becoming a teacher. He was a good teacher but I wasn't doing well in school. I kept getting in trouble in class and getting into arguments with the kids from the Reservation. Mr. Leatherman tried to talk to my folks but my father told him I was "Just a stupid kid." I liked Mr. Leatherman as a teacher even though he was strict but hated the school and hated even more the long bus trip taking me home each day. I don't know which was worse, the school or the house!

The only escape from the turmoil inside the house was spending as much time as possible exploring the desert with our German Shepard, Sabre. I had a Beagle pup for a short time but he got hurt playing in the desert and died before my parents could get him to a veterinarian in town. Sometimes I just sat on the hilltop and stared down at the city of Phoenix below, trying to imagine what other families were really like instead of those portrayed on television.

Our Laveen house had bare cement floors and no air conditioning. During the winter, a single skinny gas heater built into one corner of the living room wall heated the house. On warm summer nights, we kept the windows open. Winter and summer I always had to shake my shoes out before putting them on and could never go barefoot at night because scorpions & spiders. Daytime wasn't too bad but at night they would be crawling on the walls and floors. Sometimes I woke up with them crawling on my bed! Every time that happened I would pee in the bed for a few nights, then father would give me a whipping. Mother had another nervous breakdown that spring, so as soon as school was out I was shipped back to my grandparents again on an airplane. That made me very happy!

Mother always seemed to recover enough to put on a good show when my parents would drive back to North Carolina to pick me up at summers end. I was about to start the sixth grade and we were on the way back to Arizona, father said they were having a house built in a little town on the other side of Phoenix called Scottsdale. We would be moving into it a few days before school started. After living in that reservation house the new place was like a palace. We even had a fenced yard! In reality, it was a poorly built, tiny three bedroom two bath tract home. Immediately I thought of the possibilities for playing with other kids in the neighborhood, but that eventually changed. The land had been cattle pens for years so we had ticks and other bugs that kept coming up out of the ground for a long time after we moved into the house. The bugs were almost as bad as the house in Laveen, except no scorpions!

Motorola Electronics was building several electronic assembly plants in the area so Scottsdale went from sixteen thousand people to over thirty-five thousand people in just two years. The existing grade schools had to go on double & triple sessions because there were so many kids and sometimes we split our day between two different schools. The town was building four more elementary schools, and it looked like the classrooms would already be full the day they opened. Half way through the sixth grade Pima Elementary school was finished and opened only six blocks from our house.

After the first month or two in Scottsdale, my parents did not allow me to go outside and play with the other kids in the neighborhood. I started to call that house my 'jail'! They did not trust other families for some reason! There was always a 'rule' or 'reason' for not allowing me to socialize or play with the other kids, especially when mother was not feeling good. Mother would lay in bed for days so it quickly became my responsibility to do the laundry, ironing and house cleaning too. I spent a lot of time alone in the house, watching TV or reading books, even when mother was in her bedroom. If I did step into the backyard with the dog, there was a small bell with a string attached to it that she would ring every five minutes.

Sometimes I would sneak in friends from school when my parents were not home until one night they came home early and saw my friends running out through the back gate. The next morning father padlocked the gates before he went to work! Of course there was the usual beating at bedtime! Since we were living in town again instead of out in the boonies, I did run away a few more times, heading for Carolina and my grandmothers'. However, I was either picked up by the police or gave in and called my parents because I was stranded. Since I was being 'farmed out' so much, I kept hoping that each time would be a better living situation and nicer people. Usually not! Sometimes it was worse!

From the third grade on I was always ahead of everyone in reading & writing but behind in everything else and never could seem to catch up. I guess around the sixth grade is when I must have started believing father when he said I would always be a failure. I quit doing my school assignments and would not pay attention in class; quite often getting in trouble for talking or interrupting the class. That was back when schools allowed the teacher or the principal to paddle you, and I was paddled a lot.

Then one day the seventh grade teacher, Mr. Caldwell, tried to embarrass me in front of the class by saying that I would be a failure in life if I did not try to learn. Turning on him and yelling & crying at the same time "That's what he says all the time, so I guess it's true, I'm just a failure" and I ran out of the room. Later the Mr. Caldwell came outside and stood beside me in the shade of the building where I had been crying. He didn't say anything for a long time. He finally asked me if my dad was the person saying those things to me. I told him yes, and that he called me a "little bastard" too. I never got another paddle or reprimand for the rest of the school year!

Mr. Caldwell began helping me on my homework. He allowed me to use the school library during the study hall period, or when my other work was caught up that way I could complete my assignments. The school kept sending notes home, asking for a parent-teacher conference but they never responded. Mother was always 'sick' & father was 'too busy' to go. It was always my fault according to dad if my grades were low or I could not complete an assignment because I was not allowed to use the school library or stay after school for assistance. He would tell me that I should "Use that expensive encyclopedia I bought you."

One of my father's co-workers gave him an old 3-speed Schwinn bicycle the summer before I started eighth grade. The bike had been in a fire and needed a lot of scrubbing and repairs. It didn't have any tires or seat but the gear shifter worked. He found a used seat somewhere and bought some tires and an air pump. I didn't have a lock or chain but I had freedom! I rode that bike around the neighborhood every day, just to get out of the house. Away from the constant arguing & yelling, away from a mother that preferred to stay in bed, playing sick and continually moaning or crying. Always wanting me to bring her something and then fussing because I was not doing enough of the housework or yard work. Then when school started, things changed! The bike was stolen during the very first week of school since I didn't have a way to secure it to the bike rack. I never had another bike!

I couldn't save up any money since my parents would not allow me to have any kind of a job after school. If my grandparents sent me more than five dollars for Christmas, my parents "held" it for me. Daily chores took up most of my time, doing the family laundry and cleaning the house, tending to mother's many needs. Usually I was too tired to do my homework after dinner and would fall asleep reading. Because of my attempts to run away, father placed many restrictions on me and required that I constantly call his secretary to tell her where I was at any given moment. Then there was always the 'guilt trip' that I was obligated to take care of my bedridden mother until he returned from work.

"You can get into trouble at those things" was always the excuse, so I wasn't permitted to go to school social events. My parents always found a reason to say "No" for almost everything! As a result, I was awkward and "goofy" to just about all of my classmates, since I didn't know how to act around other people. I felt empty and afraid!

I never learned how to socialize or even laugh until I joined the army many years later.

Finally three grades at one school and no moving! Then I started the ninth grade at Scottsdale High School. That was scary! I felt so alone! What made matters worse was father's anger became more violent and he was always moody towards both my mother and me. He resented taking me to school when I was late, telling me how much of an "imposition" it caused. Yet he had to drive right by the school every morning!

The first year of high school was a very cold winter. I had to walk over two miles to school which was really not very far except that I had never had much exercise and didn't have the proper clothing for being outdoors. They wouldn't buy me a coat or heavy sweater. "You need to toughen up and be a man." Sometimes, father would say "Quit you're whining, you sound like a baby." As a result, I spent most of that winter rotating handkerchiefs between pockets and my locker, because I always had a runny nose. Occasionally if I complained a lot he would buy me antihistamines or cold medications that would dry up my nose and make me very drowsy. That stuff would cause me to fall asleep in class and then get into more trouble. I missed many fun times at school!

My freshman year I began receiving an allowance for doing the chores around the house. When I skipped lunch at the school that first semester and saved up the money to buy Christmas presents for my parents, they accused me of stealing the gifts, put me on more restrictions, and stopped my allowance. But they kept the gifts! Returning to school after Christmas vacation that year was actually a relief! I was always trying to "fix" the family problems and earn their approval. It never worked!

Changing high schools in the middle of my junior year when we moved to the northwest side of Phoenix to an area called Sunnyslope. Transferring to Sunnyslope High School was great! The school was less than a mile from the house. I was getting away from the kids that had known me for several years in Scottsdale! Maybe new classmates would not call me "goofy" or "retarded"! Slowly I started to come out of my shell. We were given study time in the library so my grades went up. I actually started making some friends but could never invite them over to our house or visit them.

During this period mother was in & out of hospitals frequently because of mental problems. She even spent a couple of months in the State Hospital in Phoenix for electroshock treatments. When mother was at home, life was difficult as I spent most of my time doing housework or taking care of her. During this period mother reconnected with the faith healing church of Christian Science and would only take her medications periodically and often refused medical care for the entire family. Learning to ignore mother's yelling & taunts by shoving my feelings deep down inside made the days easier sometimes. Later in life, I learned that was not the right thing to do! It only created more problems as I got older.

One of the neighbors was in a junior Masonic fraternity called DeMolay, and they went to meetings every two weeks in the Masonic Lodge just a few blocks from the high school. Grandfather Hays had been a high-ranking Mason in North Carolina so they figured it would be good for me to join DeMolay. Sometimes I thought it was just to get me out of the house!

DeMolay was fun and I learned a lot, discovering one important thing about myself. I could succeed at something! I was not a total failure after all! The DeMolay meetings and activities were great but I still felt like an outsider, especially when it came to social situations like the dances. I didn't know how to act around girls and there was no one to ask. Mother's answer to adolescence was to dump a stack of "questions & answers for teens" books on my bed. All the good times and enjoyable moments quickly melted away when the summer ended as I started my senior year. Life had become painful once more!

It was about three weeks before school started. We had a long vacation that summer in North Carolina as Granddad Hays was very sick; it was one of the rare trips when my parents spent a whole month together on vacation. We were driving out of town when we passed by the graveyard. Father pointed to the family cemetery plot and said, "Dane I sold your plot in the cemetery this summer. I won't allow you to be associated with this family when you die. When we get back to Phoenix, you are moving out of the house as soon as you graduate next year." That one small moment killed all the happiness I had stored up during the summer!

Feeling like an outsider, alone and unwanted in the world, my life was miserable! The school year slowly dragged by. I barely passed my classes and just did not care anymore. A couple of the teachers did take the time to talk with me or at least allow time for extra study so a few of my grades did improve but not much. Feeling so hurt inside I considered killing myself several times and did try twice but failed, chickening out at the last moment! The only bright spot was going to the DeMolay meetings! My parents never questioned or even noticed that I was in an emotional tailspin! At times it seemed they couldn't wait to get rid of me.

As graduation time approached, the 'distancing' by my parents was more apparent. The afternoon of graduation arrived and only then did they consent to go to the ceremony. I wasn't allowed to attend the prom but was permitted to go to the party afterwards, with only five dollars in my pocket. No date, no friends, no money, no car, and an early curfew. A ride was arranged, as I had to be home by 11pm. It was not a fun time!

INTERLUDE

World War II was over and our troops had come home. America began to expand. New types of industry arose and spread into the smaller towns. The United States was rebuilding after the war, retooling and growing rapidly. New technology was being introduced into everyday life and television became the center of family entertainment. Developers were building large groups of inexpensive look-a-like homes called sub-divisions on the edge of the big cities. The women that had helped with the war effort were sent back home from the factories to be mothers & housewives letting the men do the work again. The country had grown tired of the fighting and so many young men dying. Everyone wanted a fresh start, a chance to create a new life for themselves and their families.

The school kids began to feel the mood and did not want anything to do with the military. They were learning about 'The Bomb' and Communism in school. Some families were still receiving letters from the government, telling them a loved one had been lost or declared Missing in Action. Refugee children from Europe would hide when they saw someone in any type of a uniform. Their elders would speak of their previous lives in hushed tones.

A new war was beginning; called The Cold War and it was even more frightening. Russia changed from a friend to a nuclear competitor and along with China, both countries began to look beyond their borders at new territory and new conquests. The United States and many other countries developed atomic weapons and began to build large arsenals to "protect against the future." The world was changing once again.

CHAPTER SEVEN

-JIMMIE—CORTEZ, COLORADO 1946-

School days became boring for Jimmie. His family had not been poor but his parents were always frugal in their spending habits. They encouraged their children to become self-sufficient and to supplement the family income whenever possible. Jimmie's dad had died and then his mother died a short time later just as he was about to start high school. Now his sister Joan was trying to raise him, take care of the house, and pay the bills too. Sometimes they were short of stuff, but his sister never complained. Joan always had a positive attitude, and encouraged Jimmie to learn, to socialize and kept teaching him little things about their heritage as Seneca Iroquois Indians. The philosophy and attitude that Joan shared gave him strength and confidence. The teachers said he was above average in intelligence and that he should think about college. Jimmie had other things on his mind!

All through his first two years of high school, Jimmie had been against the military and any future wars. He had read about the terrible things that happened in this last war did not want his country to ever go to war again. Then there was Mott! Mott was constantly pestering him and he was becoming more and more worried that someone would find out about what he and Mott had done. Jimmie was just a kid and yet she treated him like an adult. The girls at school giggled, calling him cute because he looked so young, but Mott had treated Jimmie as if he was a grown man. Sometimes it scared him and he would have crazy dreams and wake up sweating. There was no one, not even his closest friends, or a Priest, that he felt close enough to confide in about his problems. Life was getting more complicated and confusing! What could he possibly do about the situation?

Then, the second week of October in his junior year, Mott told Jimmie she was pregnant and that her husband could not have any kids, so it had to be his baby. That put Jimmie on cloud nine and at the same time her being pregnant really scared him. What was he going to do? This was totally against the teachings of his Church! It was a Mortal Sin! Mott was a married woman! If she told her husband or anyone else that Jimmie was the father, he would be in big trouble. He was already in deep trouble in his Soul! He had skipped Confession lately because of the fear the Priest could see it in his face.

Families usually put out married women that had affairs during marriage, especially with young men! What did they do to kids that did those things? The Church had taught him that he would "go to Hell" for such a Mortal Sin. What was he going to do? Jimmie was afraid to tell his friends and now even more afraid to go to a Priest or talk to his sister. It was causing him to lose sleep at night! Occasionally he would wake up from a dream with a yell, and his sister Joan would rush into his bedroom asking if everything was okay. Lately some of his explanations had been met with her giving him that "I don't believe you look."

Jimmie didn't realize that Joan had started watching him, because she was worried that he was getting into some kind of trouble. He was becoming unusually moody and preoccupied. The young man was spending a lot of time away from home and she had found out that he was not always visiting friends as he had told her. Telling lies or hiding his activities was not normal for Jimmie. They were not raised that way!

Jimmie started having problems in school. He was constantly getting in trouble in class, and some of his grades dropped. Soon he found a part time job to keep him occupied and started saving up some money. His sister kept insisting that he stay in school and study, even if he was working. To make matters worse, one of Jimmie's best friends, Johnny Spruell, suddenly quit school saying that he "just had to get away from home." John's parents were deaf and he had endured many painful comments from his classmates over the years because his parents were "different." John did not have many friends, but he and Jimmie had hung around together for a couple of years. John was almost a year older and had stuck up for Jimmie when the other kids had teased him. He respected John and the sudden departure along with everything else made it rough.

Jimmie was depressed over Johnny leaving for weeks. Mott kept talking about divorcing her husband and marrying Jimmie when he turned 17. Would she really do that for him? What would people say, especially his sister Joan? Divorces were rare and people gossiped. Would he have to quit school and go to work full time? Would they have to leave Cortez? Suddenly Mott started slowing down the relationship between them. When he would come around after school or work, Mott would often tell him she was "too busy" to visit with him. Right after Jimmie turned 17, he went to the house and asked her when she was going to divorce her husband and marry him. Mott said that she had already told her husband that the child was his. John said he already knew about her and Jimmie. They had to end their affair immediately, and Jimmie couldn't come by the house anymore.

This hit Jimmie like a ton of bricks! He just couldn't think straight, everything in his life was suddenly turned upside down. He lost his after school job because he was "too slow" and was late for work a few too many times. Overstressed and worried he began having trouble concentrating on his homework and trying to hide his feelings from his friends and family. Jimmie felt besieged by emotions and problems that he didn't know how to handle. There wasn't anyone around he could safely ask for advice.

Jimmie was walking home from school a few weeks later when he realized Mott's house was empty. No Mott! Nothing! Managing to catch a ride out to the little airport, the ticket agent told him that John Hays moved back east somewhere on short notice. Jimmie was falling into a hole so deep, emotionally he felt like he could not crawl out. Unable to study, his grades dropped further. He just could not think clearly, life was miserable.

Finally, looking at himself in the mirror one afternoon, Jimmie thought about how his mom had always said that if you came up against a brick wall go around it. If you fall down, pick yourself up and keep on going. Squaring his shoulders, and deciding that he just had to forget about Mott and the baby, finish high school and get on with his life. Mott and the baby were beyond his control, it hurt, but it also gave him a chance to make some changes. Maybe he could still qualify for a college scholarship, if his grades were high enough.

That summer a baby boy was born in Plymouth, North Carolina to Mott. John insisted that she select the name for the baby! He wanted her to give it a name never used in the family before. Mott had wanted to name the baby James, after John's older brother. He said it was too close to "That kid's name in Cortez." A salesman visited the Farm Co-Op every month. His name was Dane, that name was acceptable to John. Several members of the family remarked about the fact it was the first dark haired baby born into the family in several generations. Everyone on both sides of the family was either blond or redheaded.

Mott was really getting emotional at times yet she would seem to bounce back overnight. John had to either return to Cortez to his airline job or go ahead and find some other type of work. The airline had only given him enough time off for Mott to have the baby. Jobs in Plymouth did not pay enough to cover their medical bills or other expenses adequately. His side jobs didn't help very much. John made the decision to move them back to Cortez and continue his job with Monarch Airlines. Cortez was a small town and the residential area was barely six blocks square. Unfortunately, the only house for rent was again within a few blocks of Jimmies' home. Maybe Jimmie would not find them! This time John would have to keep a closer eye on Mott!

Jimmie did start to pull his grades up, just as his sister started giving him lectures again about school and homework. She told him to either get back to his studies or go find a job and forget about college. Jimmie stuck it out until the end of the first semester and had decided to work part time at the hardware store and just go to school part time. Maybe he would delay graduation for another year. Many of his friends told him not to quit school or cut out so many of his classes! Then his sister found out about his idea! She would not allow Jimmie to delay graduation. Joan said there was only one way to solve the problem. She would sell off a few of the family belongings, hopefully enough to pay the mortgage off on the house. Joan would find a job in town and put off her own college plans for a semester.

As he was walking home one day Jimmie spotted Mott in the yard of the McNeill house. The McNeill family often rented the house out as they lived in another one on the other side of town. He rushed up to the gate and stopped. There was a baby boy asleep, laying on a pile of Indian blankets in the shade, while Mott pulled weeds in the yard.

Mott paused, looked into his eyes for about two minutes, and started crying. "Jimmie, this is your son, Dane. If John finds out you are here, I don't know what he will do." Astounded, Jimmie could not say a word. He just looked at that baby and broke out in a big smile. "That's my son?" She said, "Yes, I named him Dane." I'll let you visit, but you can't let John find out because he said he would beat me if he finds out we were seeing each other again." Carefully opening the gate and stepping soundlessly over to the sleeping baby, Jimmie knelt down. As he stood up the tears in his eyes contrasted sharply with the big smile on his face. Jimmie had a son!

From that day forward, Jimmie would find some excuse to stop by the house as often as possible. Always just for a few minutes on the way home from school, from work, or after seeing one of his friends in the neighborhood. No one knew why he had started smiling again, but every time Jimmie saw the baby, it made him feel good inside. He would play with the baby for a bit, maybe talk to Mott for a minute, and then quickly walk away. During the visit he was always listening out for the roar of that old motorcycle coming down the street. There had been a couple of narrow escapes as Jimmie ducked out of sight around the corner of the house when John was almost within sight of the yard. Jimmie managed to visit Dane & Mott at least every other day. He looked forward to each visit with anticipation. Afterwards, the warm feeling inside of him made up for all of the confusion and turmoil of the past.

Jimmie's grades picked back up and he quit his job at the store to concentrate on school. Joan was still worried about his behavior. Jimmie was too honest on some things and always very secretive on others. Both his mom and his sister had always been able tell when Jimmie was up to something or there was a problem. Joan didn't know what it was but something was still troubling him. However, he was doing better in school and seemed to be happy again. Perhaps he had worked through whatever problem was bothering him. At least he would graduate on time and might go on to college.

Joan quickly found a job in town and started saving up money. She managed to pay off the mortgage to the house and start a savings account for Jimmie. Then she began to make plans for the future. Joan wanted to pick up some college too, that was the only way a woman could get a decent job. Even then the pay was often lower than what men were paid for the same job.

If they sold off some of the extra furniture, closed off the unused rooms in the house, so the heating would not cost so much in the winter Jimmie could live in the house comfortably. That would bring in enough money to pay the utilities and cover his food and school expenses. Jimmie would still be able to finish high school on time. Maybe he could keep one part time job for extra spending money. Perhaps he would be lucky and qualify for that college scholarship. All Joan could do was pray that she was making the right decisions and that Jimmie would stay out of trouble. She could make plans for herself and provide for him if he would just stay focused!

They stripped the house of everything Jimmie did not need. When something was sold or a side job brought in extra money it was immediately deposited into the savings account. Joan worked a while longer and made sure a few needed minor repairs were made on the house. On the 15th of August Joan decided that she could do no more and began to pack her suitcases, the enrollment papers for college had arrived in the mail two days earlier. She left town the next day after a tearful morning of good-byes. Jimmie began his senior year of high school living alone.

Jimmie tried to convince Mott to leave her husband a couple of times, but she was too afraid of John. As often as possible, without arousing suspicion, Jimmie would drop by the house while Mott's husband was at work to play with his son for a few moments. Jimmie could not take over any toys for Dane so he spent most of the time being creative or improvising. This went on for most of the school year. Sometimes, to avoid an argument, he would wait down the street and watch until Mott would go inside the house. Then jumping over the small hedge, Jimmie would quickly hug Dane, and leave before Mott came back outside. He loved to watch Dane, even when the boy was asleep. The child was always so quiet, as if he knew Jimmie was someone special and safe. He always tried to talk to his son in a soft gentle voice. Dane would let out a gurgle and smile when he saw Jimmie.

Then it happened again! One day as Jimmie was walking down the sidewalk after school, he realized that the McNeill house was empty. The furniture, the little swing set in the yard, Mott & Dane, all gone! They had moved and Mott had never said a word. This time Jimmie knew there was nothing that he could do, no one he could talk to for advice. Knowing what they would tell him at the airport, he just went home and sat in the dark, thinking about what to do next.

Jimmie was still not legally Dane's father! There was no way to prove that Dane was his son. He went into a deep depression for a few weeks and almost quit school. Friends would come by, helping him with the house and his homework. Soon Mott & his son became a faded memory, forcefully shoved into a corner, but not forgotten. Jimmie had an empty spot in his Soul and in his heart that would not fill it up no matter how much he prayed.

Had God deserted him because of his Sin? Going to Church was difficult at times. Jimmie was afraid the Priest could see his emotions and his terrible sins! He just could not forget that little boy bundled up in that winter jump suit, standing in the yard with his hands above his head with that toothy smile. Dane was growing fast and would always break into that toothy smile when he recognized Jimmie coming into the yard. Would he remember Jimmie when he was older? Would Mott ever tell Dane the truth about his birth?

There was a good chance that Jimmie could qualify for a college scholarship in sports. If that did not work out, then he would try to go into the military. Maybe become an officer if he could qualify. A recent letter from Johnny Spruell had said it was not too bad, the food was good, and at least he got a steady paycheck. Johnny had come home on Leave and talked to Jimmie about the military. He had said that Basic Training was rough but once you completed that part of the training everything smoothed out. It was peacetime now and the military was starting to offer better pay and a variety of jobs. Right before Johnny returned to duty he had Jimmie take a photo of him and his sister Zola standing in front of the family car. Johnny looked sharp in that uniform!

Every day Jimmie checked the mailbox when he got home, hoping for a letter from Mott but she never wrote him. The scholarship came through in April, he wrote his sister about the good news. Opening up the envelope and reading the good news made him so happy that he ran down the street shouting that he was going to college. Life was getting better perhaps there was hope!

Meanwhile, Joan had made the decision that after college she would become a Nun. She would wait and tell Jimmie when he was settled at school and doing okay in his classes. Ever since her parents died, she could not fill the emptiness inside. She prayed about it constantly. Service to the Church seemed to be the answer! Putting away one's past, pains, and bad memories might just fill that cold emptiness inside of her. The Order of St. Francis offered a series of opportunities around the world and they had openings at their Convent. She prayed that maybe she could find some happiness in her life with what they offered.

Joan met with one of the Convent representatives and discovered that there was another alternative. If she did not want to wait, Joan could join the Convent and once her probationary training was over, she could return to college to complete her degree, with the Church paying for the rest of her education as long as she kept her grades up. However, joining the Convent also meant Joan would not be able to keep in contact with Jimmie while she was in the probationary period. Would he be okay? Could he take care of himself? This path appealed to Joan as going to college had proved more expensive than expected. She still worried about Jimmie. Could he really handle everything, and still graduate from high school. If he could keep his grades up and qualify for a college scholarship it would give him a chance for a good life.

Receiving the letter a few days later from Jimmie, telling her that he had been awarded the sports scholarship was all Joan needed. A heavy weight had been lifted from her shoulders. Her prayers were answered. Now she was free to make decisions regarding her own future! Becoming an instant parent when their mother died had kept Joan from enjoying her high school days. There was always the feeling that she had missed some things in life because of the sudden family responsibilities.

Joan made a phone call to the Convent, set up appointments with her instructors and the college admission office and began to close out her affairs. At the end of the semester she left college, boarding the bus for Milwaukee, Wisconsin a few days later. She gazed out the window as the mountains surrounding Greely, Colorado slowly shifted into the plains. Would she ever return to Cortez? Joan decided that it was time to start a new chapter in her life as she exited the bus and entered the Convent.

-INTERLUDE-1950

In a place far away on the other side of world, the Chinese had been helping a little country on their border, called Korea. They called it "helping" but what they were really doing was making soldiers out of farmers and causing a rebellion against the Korean government. The Russians, also seeing an opportunity, offered to supply equipment and training officers in exchange for setting up military bases along the border. Soon both countries began sending more equipment and troops into Korea above objections from other countries. Sometimes the troops, services, and equipment from the two countries were combined. The Korean leaders often found that they had no choice in the decision making or movement of the Chinese & Russian military units.

The United States and the newly formed United Nations Council began to warn Korea about its military buildup. Then the reinforced rebel military began to fight the Korean National government forces and slowly advanced towards the sea. The United Nations threatened military action and asked the United States to assist. The United States began to train the Army and Air Force for another war.

After much debate, decisions were made at the United Nations. The Korean rebels along with the governments of China & Russia ignored the UN pleas. Under the direction of the United Nations an invasion fleet with soldiers and equipment landed at Incheon Korea. Their plan was to provide military aid to the legitimate government of Korea. Once again, American soldiers bid their families farewell and went off to fight in a foreign land. Once more American men died in combat or returned home from war injured and maimed.

CHAPTER EIGHT

-Going to War in Korea-

The United Nations called it a "police action." Many American Soldiers began to die and the Air Force had begun to build up bases on nearby islands, in preparation for fighting this growing threat that seemed more like a war than a "police action." Private John Spruell joined several thousand other soldiers bound for Korea. Once the troop ship arrived in Korea, he was going to be sent as a replacement to the 57th Field Artillery Battalion which was part of the 7th Infantry Division.

PVT John Spruell was looking at all of the other soldiers crowded onto the troop ship, thinking this sure looked like plain old war and he had dropped right in the middle of it! They had been at sea for only a week, but it seemed like it was forever. There was nowhere to go on board the ship, without stepping over someone or to have a moment's privacy. This was the first time he had ever been on the ocean and it was lousy! John spent most of his time writing letters, looking out to sea, and wondering what his folks were doing. He had asked his sister Zola not to be afraid to ask for help if things got rough. Their parents were so stubborn at times!

Zola Spruell receives a letter from John.

-July 1950-Japan-

"Dear Zola,

I hope this letter finds everybody at home in good health. I am writing a few lines to let you know how things are going. I don't know if I will ever get that jacket you are wanting. I am moving out of this camp and we are headed for Korea. I may not get a chance to see home again. I am sure that I have to fight. From what I hear, it is a little hard going in Korea. So if I don't ever make it home take care of mother. Don't tell mother!! I think I will make it home. I feel lucky. Well anyway wish me luck. If I can I will try and write to you while I am in Korea. Well I can't think of anything else to say so I will close. Your Brother, Johnny"

-September 1950-Japan-

"Dear Sis,

I received your letter. I am now in the day room trying to answer it. Well, there isn't much to write about. It is just the same old story every day. We are going to have two inspections Saturday. I hope I can pass them. I have been here in Japan almost two months and haven't got a pass to go to town yet. It is harder to get pass now that we are on the deck. Whenever I go to town I will look for that jacket you are wanting.

Well it won't be long now and I will be nineteen. That will mean I have two years to do over here. It's raining out now, has been raining all day. This is the rainy season. It sure is quiet here in the barracks now. Everybody went to the beer hall. It usually is noisy in here. It sure would be nice to have a little peace. Maybe I can get a little sleep before they get back and start making more noise. I'll close for now. Your Brother, Johnny"

-October 1950-Korea-

"Dear Zola,

I received your letter yesterday so I am writing you one now. This is the first chance I have had to write a letter since I have been in Korea and I am telling you one thing that I am sure not having any fun over here. Having these North Koreans taking pot shots at me is sure no fun. Oh well one good thing is that I am still here and not six foot under. When I get back to the States, that is if I ever get back to the States I am going to stay in the army three more years and try to go to Germany. This Japan & Korea is all messed up. I am going to see if Germany is any worse than Japan. I didn't know it could get so cold as it is here in Korea. I am on a ship now. I have been on it for two weeks now and the ship still hasn't moved yet. Since I have been in the army I think I have spent half of it on the water. I have a long time yet to go in this army. Then I might not get out when my time is up, with all this fighting going on.

Ted Baskett wrote me and said he was drafted into the army. He said he was going to Fort Riley where I went to take Basic. I got a letter from mother and she said she liked it in Wichita and that she was happy there where she lived. Well I got to go to chow so I will close for now. Your Bro, Johnny

PS: Another thing is this army is about to starve me to death. I was a cook once until I got put out. I suppose I was eating too much when I was cooking. I am now on a 105 Howitzer. I am a number two man. I am the man that puts the shell into the gun. The only thing I dislike about the gun is it makes too much noise when it goes off and hurts my ears."

—57TH FIELD ARTILLERY BATTALION—

PVT Spruell didn't have much of a chance to relax upon his arrival at the staging area in Korea. As soon as he reported to his unit he was assigned to a series of work details moving supplies and delivering them to other military units along the Korean coastline. Sometimes it felt like they were going in circles because units might change location and they would arrive to find no one willing to accept the supplies. In between the deliveries he underwent additional weapons and combat training. Eventually his unit was ordered into action, as the 7th Infantry Division had been ordered to go on the offensive against the Communist soldiers. They would launch a counterattack on the 15th of September. Once again PVT John Spruell stood on a ship and wished he was back in Cortez. As the ships reached the edge of the beachhead, several destroyers were bombarding the coastline with their heavy cannons. The troop ships hadn't moved up to the staging area yet but still the sound of the heavy guns was deafening.

Finally, the convoy came within sight of the Korean shoreline at Inchon. Soldiers checked their gear and prepared to board the landing craft (LST), his Platoon Leader, LT. Johnson, came by collecting all of the letters that everyone had written. The Lieutenant was making small talk, trying to ease the tension. John's turn came to climb into the LST and once again he felt like a sardine crammed into a can. Some men were praying, some stared at the beach and others avoided eye contact. Everyone was scared but only a few men admitted it. John had mixed feelings; he was ready to fight but worried that he would not be ready when they landed on the beach. Oddly, his apprehension disappeared when the landing craft stopped and the steel gate of the landing craft crashed into the water. He began to wade through the low tide towards the sandy beach of Inchon.

The 57th Field Artillery Battalion was held back from immediately going into action because the 105MM Howitzers arrived late since the Navy had loaded them on a different ship. Once the equipment was unloaded and everyone was ready, the order was given to proceed into combat the first week of October. The first assigned task was to set up their Howitzers on the runway of the Suwon air field and provide artillery support as needed by the newly formed 31st Regimental Combat Team (RCT). It was not until late November before PVT John Spruell saw heavy combat action.

As they neared a small village the soldiers were involved in an intense battle with heavy casualties. Everyone had to dig into the hillside and wait while the tanks and the sporadic air support fighters tried to shake the enemy loose. John watched as wounded men passed him by, heading for the nearby temporary aid station. Sometimes they would pass the body of a soldier, lying on the roadside and John would have to force himself to look away. He wasn't like some of the soldiers! Death bothered him, especially when he saw the twisted bodies and faces of men that he knew! The Graves Registration Platoon had already dug several mass graves and was following the advancing combat line, digging more as needed. It had started to rain again, they were predicting more rain for tomorrow, and it sure felt cold enough for snow.

The tanks and infantry began to move forward and the call went out for the troops and equipment to follow them. Acrid smoke from the exhaust of tanks & trucks hung in the air as PVT John Spruell's Battery 'B' packed up their gear and prepared to move. Once everything was ready the order was given to load up and John climbed up into the truck. Tightening his ammo belts and checking his rifle as he sat down. John's artillery battalion would follow the battle until ordered to set up their guns once again.

The new mission for the artillery battalion was to cross the mountains and hold a large reservoir called "Chosin" and the small villages around it with their 105MM cannon. The Air Force wanted to use one of the valleys as a landing strip and staging area. The allied forces had to prevent the Chinese from coming through the mountain pass and into the lowlands below. It was a hard time fighting their way up the mountain road that led away from the beaches. Thick sticky mud was everywhere! The air felt like it was getting colder every hour. John was guessing that a big winter storm was building.

As the soldiers crested the mountain range, the winding dirt road was already slick with ice and snow. Daytime temperatures were dropping, the nights were always well below zero. The convoy of men and equipment reach the top of the mountain pass and began the slow decent towards the Chosin Reservoir. Another storm would just make the road even more deadly! Snipers hidden on the hilltops behind boulders or dug into the mountainside would fire at them and then disappear. During an intense period of fighting that morning, John's squad leader was shot and killed. Lieutenant Johnson told John Spruell that now he was promoted to Private First Class (PFC) and that he was to be the new squad leader. As PFC John Spruell took over the squad the long convoy began to move forward again. The sky darkened and the cold gusts of wind cut right through his coat, most of the men in John's battalion lacked enough cold weather gear to adequately protect them. This wasn't going to be easy!

From John's point of view the enemy seemed to keep retreating in front of them. Then they would suddenly stop to put up a fight, each time inflicting heavy casualties on the American forces. The weather just kept getting worse. Equipment began to freeze up along with the men. The mountain roads were slowly narrowing and every truck or tank that passed by just left a deeper hole in the mud. Some men, too tired to walk anymore, would sit down on the roadside to rest for a minute. Later someone would come along, try to wake the man up, only to realize that the soldier had frozen to death right where he sat. Sometimes the dead couldn't be buried, as the ground was often frozen solid or too rocky. Attempts to transport dead & wounded back over the mountain often resulted in more tragedy.

Within two weeks, rations and ammunition were in short supply. Frequent obstructions would tie up the troops for hours, usually caused by trucks breaking down or the seemingly impassable terrain or land mines. Food served hot would develop an icy frost within minutes because the air was so cold. Due to enemy artillery fire, snipers, roadblocks, or landslides, the supplies of food clothing

& ammunition began to run short for everyone. Every day was becoming a grueling fight for survival!

PFC John Spruell's battalion began to experience equipment failures because of the snow and extreme cold temperatures. All of the soldiers were starting to get sick. Most of the men were suffering frostbite because they were short on cold weather gear. Men used newspapers & rags to wrap their feet in an attempt to keep warm. Their uniforms offered little protection from the cold and biting wind. The enemy appeared to be dressed just as poorly to survive the cold weather! At times they could be seen looting American corpses or supplies. The Chinese and Korean soldiers were required to "live off the land" so their supplies were minimal. Some of the American equipment had not been designed for this type of cold weather combat. Eventually orders were given by the senior commanders that rather than allow the enemy to utilize American supplies & equipment, it would be burned. This even included food and clothing.

Unknown to the Allied & US Commanders, their troops were slowly being drawn into a trap. For every mile that they advanced, more Communist Chinese & North Korean Forces slowly and quietly began to encircle them. Breaks in the advancing column of troops & equipment, often caused by mud and equipment failures provided opportunities for the Chinese. The enemy forces would use these situations to set up their own roadblocks and traps. The Chinese began to systematically kill the American soldiers, always picking off the officers and NCOs first, and then destroying any equipment so it would further block the roadway.

As the Allied forces advanced, whole sections were sometimes cut-off from each other, and communications began to breakdown. Each of the Allied Generals had their own idea on how to proceed, and they could not agree on a quick solution. They were still using combat tactics learned in Europe during World War II, which did not work with this type of fighting. Meanwhile, their troops were dying or being captured! A soldier would wake up in the morning, to find the man next to him dead with his throat cut. Morale was low;

they had not been trained to deal with this type of psychological warfare.

The Chinese/Korean forces periodically used portable public address systems playing loud music and battle cries that kept the American soldiers from sleeping. Carefully prepared speeches were broadcast over the speaker systems spread through the hills or on transport vehicles. This was designed to create doubt and fear amongst the allied soldiers or to lure them into the open and sometimes it worked. Despite many problems the American commanders tried to keep military discipline, even in the harshest of conditions. Often the commanders held inspection formations just to keep the soldiers occupied. Meanwhile the roads became nothing more than frozen rutted dirt trails as they led down the mountain into the valleys surrounding a large reservoir known as "Chosin."

Battery B, 57th Field Artillery Battalion of the 7th US Infantry slowly moved their 105MMs and equipment down the mountain towards the little village of Hagaru-ri; it was a windy and cold morning. PFC Spruell's feet were numb, possibly early frostbite. All the members of his squad had the same problem. Some of the men began to complain that their fingers were numb too. There was nothing more Spruell could do to help his men fight the cold! The Battalion's backup supply of clothing was already depleted or destroyed. There was no more clothing or blankets to help fight the cold. There was no way to send any of the soldiers back down the mountain.

The truck they had been riding in broke an axle, so now they were walking in the snow and did not have any dry socks or boots. A small Marine Detachment with Navy Corpsmen had set up an Aid Station a few miles down the road. Perhaps the Aid Station could do something for John Spruell and his fellow soldiers. Maybe they would have a chance for some warm food and dry clothes. A warm bath would be great. Hot coffee would be better!

The 5th Marine Detachment finally arrived in their designated area to support the Army and create an airfield. Only to find the army convoy mired down in the middle of mud and confusion. Where were they supposed to set up their defense lines? Who was in charge? There was no leadership, no coordination. Daytime snipers and nightly attacks left some soldiers demoralized, and there was nowhere to go. Suddenly the various commanders realized too late, there was little or no communication between the military units. Some of the commanders and their staff had even been cut off from their own troops or killed by ambush, artillery, or advancing enemy troops. The remaining commanders from some of the various forces actually argued with each other over who was supposed to be in command. It was total chaos!

As a result, there was no way to provide relief troops or assistance to the various units in and around the Hagaru-ri village and the surrounding valley. Previous reports had said the Hagaru-ri area was entirely safe, totally under Allied military control yet this was obviously incorrect. There were still active mine fields alongside many of the roads causing havoc with soldiers and equipment. The C-47 & C-119 supply planes would drop ammunition & food for the soldiers only to learn later that the wind had blown some of the parachutes with the supplies into enemy hands just a short distance away. Another air drop was unsuccessful as the aircraft flew over the wrong area resulting in the supplies once again falling into enemy hands. The 57th Field Artillery Battalion wasn't receiving all of its supplies, including needed ammunition.

Many of the officers & NCOs died as the Chinese slowly encircled the mountains around the reservoir, tightening the circle more each day. There were now over 60,000 enemy soldiers surrounding the Chosin region. The UN soldiers were quickly becoming disheartened and some began to scatter due to the lack of guidance. The military forces had not only become surrounded by the enemy but the enemy had split the Allied forces into so many small groups that they were unable to properly function. Nighttime attacks by the enemy left little time for sleep. What appeared to be a safe spot for defense during the daytime had become a deadly battleground during the night. It became apparent to all concerned they would have to fight their way out of the various valleys and villages without help, without direction and possibly without hope.

Only a few of the front line officers had anticipated and prepared for a major engagement with the enemy. Captain James McClymont, commander of D Battery, 15th Antiaircraft Artillery had become part of the 7th Infantry Division's 31st Regimental Combat Team (RCT) on 24 November. His mission was to provide automatic antiaircraft fire to support the 31st RCT attack on Chosin. They had only two days to plan their mission and travel almost 100 kilometers over the snow & ice covered dirt roads with subzero temperatures. Prior to his arrival at the Chosin Reservoir CPT McClymont had made sure all of his platoons had double their basic load of ammunition. This precaution eventually saved many lives.

Because of his foresight, Captain McClymont's forces managed to fight off a serious attack killing over 200 Chinese soldiers. His actions prevented the 57th Field Artillery Battalion from being totally wiped out during that attack. The enemy made several more advances which were rebuffed, with high casualties on both sides. However, by December 1st after four days of intense fighting, and limited re-supply, they were almost out of ammunition and fuel. His soldiers attempted to protect a 30-vehicle convoy of wounded soldiers and failed because the Chinese had set up a road block and the entire convoy was destroyed. Fortunately Captain McClymont was able to lead the remainder of his troops in a daring assault, overrunning some of the Chinese positions. His small group made it to safety and joined the Marine Detachments at Hagaru-Ri. The 31st RCT had started with 3,000 men but only 385 reached Hagaru-ri.

When Commander of the US Army 7th Inf. Division, General Hodes, flew out of Hagaru-ri airfield on December 2, he did not know that the majority of his soldiers were already dead, dying, captured, or surrounded by the enemy. Battery A of the 57th had been overrun by the Chinese on the night of 27-28 November; most of the survivors were merged with Battery B or other nearby units. Nevertheless, Battery B engaged the enemy the following night, with equally devastating results.

PFC Spruell's entire 57th Field Artillery Battalion had already lost nearly all of its equipment and ammunition by the first day of December due to continuous fighting and equipment failures. Their commander ordered them to destroy any usable equipment that they had to be left behind so the enemy could not use it against them later. Retreat was impossible! Moving forward was sure death! The weather was getting worse; more men were dying from the subzero cold.

As the survivors and wounded straggled into the little base controlled by the Marine Detachment, an attempt was made to airlift out the wounded with small planes using the airfields at Yonpo and Hagaru-ri. Without a solid line of defense, the Chinese & Korean forces could easily overrun the entire area. Several of the Marine offices took charge of the situation, sending some of the army troops over to the east side of the valley, attempting to set up a defensive line in that direction. Someone had to take leadership responsibility!

The Chinese began to close the trap on 5 December. Over 1,500 wounded troops from the 7th Division were safely airlifted from the tiny Hagaru-ri airfield. Around 400 members of the 7th Infantry Division remained behind that were physically able to fight even though many of them were injured or suffering from frost bite. They joined other Allied units to create a single fighting force with LTC Berry K. Anderson of the 7th Marine Regiment taking command. At this point, survival was more important than the branch of service!

General O.P Smith, Commander of the1st Marine Division, ordered the airfield runway lengthened so that larger aircraft could fly in for evacuating troops. He was anticipating the need for a full scale evacuation. His men had just begun to work when they realized their actions were too little, too late. Their position at the airfield was about to be overrun by the enemy and they had to quickly change their plans again. The 1st Marine Division became the last line of defense as more Army & Marine soldiers continued to fight their way down into the valley from the mountainsides. The valleys and hillsides around the Chosin Reservoir were littered with dead and pockets of men fighting to stay alive. The trap was closing fast! The Allied forces were facing massacre. The combined forces attempted to breakout of Hagaru-ri and the surrounding valleys on 6 December.

On the morning of 6 December 1950, Private First Class John Spruell and the few remaining members of his unit were in the middle of the Hagaru-ri valley. The soldiers were trapped, powerless to reach the Navy Aid Station. It was impossible for them to join the group of soldiers that was going to attempt the breakout. It was very cold and the blowing snow hampered their vision, most of them had minor injuries. A few men were seriously injured, desperately needing medical attention. The mud and ice made it difficult to move the remainder of their equipment much less themselves.

Several men made it across part of the frozen reservoir to safety. Others fell through weak spots in the ice and died. Some men died, others were severely injured by land mines placed around the reservoir. Chinese & Korean snipers shot at anyone lucky enough to find solid ground as the snow covered terrain and frozen ground prevented several soldiers from finding adequate shelter. Many soldiers were the victims of land mines buried on the roadside. Some men just froze to death where they sat, weapons in hand. PFC John Spruell of Cortez, Colorado died that day. The Navy Aid Station might have been able to save his life if he could have gotten to it in time.

CHAPTER NINE

JIMMIE—CORTEZ-APRIL 1951

Jimmie received a letter from Joan telling him about Johnny Spruell's death on the 20th of March during his first year of college. Upon receipt of the telegram stating that John had died in Korea his parents had refused to accept his death. Because they were deaf and there were only a few people in town that could understand their sign language they tended to isolate themselves from other folks in Cortez. They did not have a telephone or anyway to use one if it had been available. As a result, some of the people in town did not understand the situation, shunning them just because they "were different." The Spruell family did not want to believe that John was dead, yet they continued to receive letters marked "Individual Deceased" returned in the mail, a long time after Johnny had died. His parents just went on with their lives, never asking anyone for help and only telling a few folks about the letters from the army.

Jimmie was tormented and confused! He felt torn between loyalties and emotions! What was he going to do? His world was falling apart around him. Johnny had been his best friend! He has

93

always been against another war, yet felt the need to avenge Johnny! He felt angry and did not understand why! Mott has gone away with his son and he has no chance of ever seeing them again. Then, there is Abby, a girl he had met at the college and started dating. They have been talking about a possible engagement. What about his promises to her? Abby is such a wonderful person, Jimmie could be happy with her! Maybe he would even be able to forget about Mott & Dane. Should he tell Abby about Mott and Dane? Decisions, apprehension, and confusion!

The first day of April Jimmie woke up determined to make some changes in his life. On the way home from school Jimmie stopped by the military recruiting office and spoke with a recruiter about job and education choices in the military. It doesn't sound so bad, he thought, Johnny seemed to like it. The Recruiting office gave Jimmie a lot of information and made several suggestions. Because of his college and test scores, he could join the Air Force and leave later in the week if he wanted to. By the time Jimmie made it home that afternoon he had made up his mind. He quickly wrote a letter to the school, planning to drop it off at the admissions office early in the morning. The decision was made; he would give up his scholarship and go down to enlist in the Air Force tomorrow!

Five days later Jimmie woke up early and had a quick breakfast before he went back to the recruiting office for final processing. He had chosen the job of Tail Gunner for the B-29 bomber. After everyone was sworn in later that day, Jimmie was allowed to go home for a few hours to complete the arrangements with the bank for the sale of the house and to close out his personal affairs. The remaining time was spent writing tearful letters to his sister Joan & Abby. Jimmie managed to send Mott a couple of letters before he left Cortez. She had finally replied so he knew her and the baby were okay. Would he ever see them again?

That evening Jimmie boarded a train for San Antonio, Texas to begin basic training at Lackland Air Force Base. So many men had enlisted because of the Korean War that Jimmie and many others were required to temporarily live in large tents while they underwent their initial training at Lackland. Jimmie was fortunate; he only spent a week in a giant tent before shifting into the wooden barracks. After Basic, they would go on to Gunnery School & Flight School at Lowry AFB and then to Randolph AFB near San Antonio for Combat Crew Training and graduation.

As training progressed, the number of students in each class began to dwindle. Several of Jimmie's classmates failed the Survival Training course at Camp Carson, Colorado. Others could not pass weapons training or the final flight physical exams. Jimmie seemed to thrive on the challenge and regimentation. It kept his mind occupied and he enjoyed the classes. By the time he finished his studies each night he would fall sound asleep very fast. Fellow classmates would sometimes joke that Jimmie definitely slept like a log. It was difficult to wake him up in the mornings.

Graduation day at Randolph AFB finally arrived. After the ceremony, crewmembers posed in front of their B-29 for a group photograph. Jimmie mailed his brother & sister copies of the graduation photo. He also took a chance, sending a copy to Mott in Prescott with a short letter. When they had first started flight school training Jimmie would look at those giant B-29 bombers lined up on the parking apron and wonder how could such monsters fly. Now the airplanes no longer appeared to be so large and overpowering, they were old friends. He liked flying and the Air Force was teaching him a lot, perhaps he would make it a career.

Over the next several weeks, the crew flew their plane around the country to different Air Force bases, undergoing specialized training and becoming more proficient in their navigation techniques. They were due to return to Lake Charles Air Force Base in Louisiana tomorrow for their final preparations and training before flying to Kadena AFB in Okinawa. He had finally made up his mind on a few things! Jimmie wanted to concentrate on his job as a tail gunner without having to worry over personal problems. Nor did he want to end up like Johnny Spruell, having folks suffer needlessly because of his death!

Upon arrival at Lake Charles AFB, an officer gave daily briefings on what to expect on the trip overseas, their arrival in Okinawa, and about the various procedures when they began their bombing missions in Korea. There was very little free time for any of the crewmembers. Every waking moment of the day was busy with preparations and training for final departure. To his surprise, Jimmie received a letter from Joan the last week of training. The Convent had given permission for her to visit and say good-by. Joan had not approved of him leaving school and joining the Air Force but she said that he was old enough to make his own decisions and she would support him in his choices.

She and Abby would be driving down to see him on the weekend before the B-29 squadron departed for Kadena. As each day passed during that week, Jimmie was constantly thinking about what he wanted to say to Abby and how upset she might be over the situation. He was seriously considering telling Abby that they couldn't get married and that she needed to find someone else. He didn't want her to wait for him to return from the war! He might not come back!

Saturday morning Jimmie woke up before the alarm. It had been a rough night with very little sleep. He was at the mess hall for breakfast at 6a.m. then back to the barracks waiting anxiously for the phone call from the front gate that visitors had arrived. By 8am he was tired of looking out the window in his room so he walked downstairs to the dayroom. Jimmie sat sipping his sixth cup of coffee and staring at the clock on the wall of the day room. At 9:15am, the dayroom phone on the nearby wall rang. By this time, Jimmie was very nervous and he jumped out of his seat to answer the phone, spilling his coffee on the table. Luckily it didn't splash onto his uniform and he hurriedly wiped it up. They were here! Was he ready for all this? Would he be able to tell Abby how he felt?

Walking up to the gate, Jimmie saw both women standing by the car talking with the guard. Joan was wearing her usual dark dress & blouse with a sweater but Abby had on a white & pink sundress that made her long dark hair stand out. A warm breeze was blowing, Abby smiled as she held the edge of her billowing skirt. He gave

Joan a quick hug and a kiss on the cheek, then grabbing Abby, gave her a long kiss and hug. Jimmie held onto Abby for a minute, not wanting to let go. This was not going to be easy but he had to do it! Realizing that he loved her very much! Would he be able to go through with his plans?

They spent most of the day trading gossip about friends in Cortez and talking about his training at the base. Joan said very little about life at the Convent, other than the fact it kept her very busy. Both women avoided talking about Korea and the war. Finally, as the afternoon ended, Joan & Abby were going to have to leave shortly. Taking a deep breath, almost forcing his voice to be steady, Jimmie said he needed to talk to Abby alone for a moment. Joan walked over to the fence to watch the airplanes while they talked. She had an uneasy feeling that it was going to be a long ride home that night.

Abby said, "You look worried, like something has been on your mind all day." Jimmie took another deep breath, putting his arm around her shoulder and said "Abby I need you to understand something. I don't know what the future holds, with this war and everything going on." "I know Jimmie" "No, let me finish Abby, I need to say this now or I won't be able to say it at all. I don't want you to wait for me to return, we don't know what will happen or if I will even return. You have a good future ahead of you when you finish college. Go find a smart man to marry. One that will take care of you, love you, and give you a nice home and family. And know that I'll always have a special spot in my heart for you."

Abby looked at him with tears in her eyes. "I had hoped you were going to ask me to marry you before you left. I thought we were a sure thing! I love you and am willing to wait, no matter what the outcome, even if you come home injured." By this time, Jimmie had started to choke up; there were tears in his eyes too. "Abby I mean it! I don't want you to wait for me. War changes people, if I do come home without injury I still won't be the same person you knew. You deserve a better life than I can give you right now. I want you to go home and not be concerned about me anymore."

With that, Jimmie turned and walked over to Joan who was still standing by the fence. "I love you Sis, take care of yourself, and I'll try to write when I can. I've just told Abby that we can't get married and that she needs to find someone else. So you might want to take her home now." Giving Joan a tearful hug, he turned away from her, hastily walking down the sidewalk towards the barracks. Jimmie was never to see either of them again.

-INTERLUDE-

The bloody battle of the Chosin Reservoir is over. The Air Force continues their bombing runs with B-29s concentrating on destroying bridges, dams, and railways. Targeting anything industrial that could slow the enemy down or stop their attempt to take over the small country of Korea. The loss of men and machines on both sides of the war is staggering. Political negotiations through the United Nations slowly progress despite Russia & China continuing to supply men and equipment to the Korean army while systematically stalling the talks in the United Nations Assembly. The Korean rebel leaders have taken over control of the country and forced the legitimate government to go into exile. The UN forces have suffered several devastating defeats on the ground.

The bombing missions over Korea are becoming more hazardous every day due to new MiG fighter jets & equipment supplied by China and Russia. As the B-29s return from each bombing mission, the losses increase and new replacement personnel merged with seasoned crews upon arrival. Damaged planes were scavenged for spare parts to repair those still able to fly on a daily basis. Just like World War II, families receive the dreaded telegram or letter telling of a loved one lost in combat. The United Nations "police action" seemed more like a full blown war!

CHAPTER TEN

PRESCOTT, ARIZONA 1951-1952

Mott & John had moved to the small mountain town of Prescott in northern Arizona. The commercial aviation business was booming, new routes were added, and some companies merged and grew, some failed. Monarch Airlines merged becoming Frontier Airlines. John was working as a counter & ramp agent, wearing the newly designed grey with brown trim Frontier Airlines uniform. Housing was so limited in the area that the airfield employees were required to live in old metal Quonset huts located near the air terminal. The huts had been quickly converted into duplex apartments. Having a metal shell they were cold in the winter and hot in the summer. John & Mott lived in the hut next to the old Chinese railroad workers cemetery from the late 1800s. It was lonely there, but at least she had a few neighbors to talk to and Dane could play with some toddlers his own age. John spent a lot of time working and even volunteered for the local Civil Air Patrol activities.

All of these activities combined kept them busy and neither one would discuss what had happened in Cortez. If Mott did bring up the subject, John quickly silenced her! Secretly Mott kept worrying about Jimmie. She had even sent him a letter giving him their new address but told him not to write, as she did not want John to find out. He did anyway, even including his flight school graduation photo with the names of all the crewmembers. Mott was afraid John might see the letters so she kept them hidden in a place he would never look. Stuck between some old magazines she was saving that had pictures of fancy homes. Maybe someday, Mott wished, she would have a nice home like those in the magazines.

Just before they moved to Prescott, Mott went into the hospital with what the doctors said was a "nervous breakdown." John sent Dane to live with her sister & parents in North Carolina. Her parents (the Jacksons) had finally moved from the old wooden frame house into a new brick home with extra bedrooms so there was always plenty of room. John's parents (the Hays) lived on their farm just three miles down the road. Dane was home again with Mott, he was always asking when his grandmother would be coming to visit. The boy was learning to talk fast! Sometimes John would ponder, noting that when Dane was gone their marriage seemed to be better and Mott was not so moody. Every time Dane came home Mott would have crying spells. Probably thinking about that kid in Cortez!

The newly formed Bonanza Airlines purchased the northern Arizona route from Frontier Airlines and John changed uniforms once more. The shoebox where he kept important papers was getting full but John felt the need to keep every little receipt or letter. Quite the opposite of Mott's constant state of disorganization! At least there was a small pay increase this time. He could actually save some money each month. If Mott didn't get sick again!

Mott had her good days and bad ones too. John would be mad at her for a day or two over some little thing, then try to make up for it. Every time he walked in the door, she was afraid he would hit her. At least John didn't hurt Dane, but he did ignore the boy most of the time. That was just as bad!

Finally, John decided that they needed to move away from the airport so the other employees would not see Mott when she had emotional problems. He told her that she embarrassed him! Prescott was a very small town with few choices but he found a small stone cottage in the foothills of the Prescott Dells in mid-March.

The cottage belonged to one of the local pioneer families that had homesteaded the land during the last century. The narrow dirt road by the house was heavily lined with Ponderosa Pine trees. Only one family lived nearby so there was very little traffic. Their four boys were already teenagers and always kept occupied and the family did not seem to gossip. In many ways, the stone cottage was nicer than the Quonset hut but it was isolated!

Mott could plant a garden in one corner of the front yard and there was plenty of room for Dane to play outside. Unfortunately, it had only one bedroom so they had to share the one bed and John did not like that. When it came time for bed, John always insisted that Dane sleep facing the wall. Soon Mott even lost interest in the garden she had started or keeping the house clean. Without people around to talk with and keep her busy, Mott began to think about Jimmie and the war in Korea.

She started to have emotional problems again, unable to handle even the simplest housekeeping chore. This time John's sister-in-law Delores came up from Phoenix and helped with Dane and the house for a month. His brother Bill was a pilot for Frontier Airlines and they had a very nice home in Phoenix. The stress and worry over things was too much for Mott and she went into the hospital again. Delores took Dane to live with her family in Phoenix for three months. John just kept working. He periodically visited Mott at the hospital, never staying very long.

Mott finally came home from the hospital and Delores brought Dane back to Prescott. John found another house, a few miles closer to work. It was an old wooden house behind the drive-in theatre in Prescott. The windows rattled in the wind and the house was always dusty. It was in an open grazing range area with Brahma cows that would walk right into the yard. Sometimes the cows pushed right through the small picket fence around the front door which would scare Mott and she would start crying.

Her personality had changed so much! When they were kids, Mott always seemed so fearless, even going squirrel hunting in the swamp by herself. Now she seemed to be afraid of the least little thing. Dane was growing a little bit, but he always seemed to be sick. At times things seemed to be getting better between Mott and John. Mott kept trying to find a way to be happy. They made friends with some of the new airport employees and began having parties in the airport hangar. They would just wrap Dane up in a blanket and lay him in a corner.

John was making an effort to be nicer to Mott. Managing to save up enough money to buy and old Ford Model-A painted a bright lemon yellow. They began to socialize once again with neighbors and coworkers from the airport. Sometimes they would bundle Dane up in the rumble seat and go for a ride in the hills just to get out of the house. Mott liked it when John drove fast on the narrow winding mountain roads! John started taking them camping in the surrounding forest on the weekends, it was a good stress reliever for him too. A chance to get away from the office and Mott seemed to enjoy the camping.

During one of the weekend camping in the Prescott Dells, Dane was sleeping on the Model-A seat while John & Mott slept in their sleeping bags by the camp fire, a large mountain lion walked through the camp. They didn't even know it until they saw the footprints in the sand near their sleeping bags the next morning during breakfast. The next day the local newspaper had a picture of a record size mountain lion shot that same night near the campground. The mountain lion had the misfortune of exploring a camp where there were several guns readily available. John decided it was time to get a dog for protection. Finding no adult dogs available that were safe around toddlers, he settled on a newly weaned Cocker Spaniel pup named Pepper.

Then the letter came! It was a cool November morning, Mott had just voted for Eisenhower that week. Her "I like Ike" sticker was still on the refrigerator door. She was feeling good and had spent the morning putting a henna rinse on her long auburn hair to make it a deeper red. The envelope was from the Department of The Air Force, addressed to Mott. Fortunately, John was still at work. With trembling hands, she sat Dane down on the couch beside her, telling him to be still while she opened the letter. The first words she read were "We regret to inform you" and she started crying. By the time John arrived home Mott was tightly curled up in bed, sobbing and moaning. The letter still firmly clutched in her hand. Dane was crawling around the house in soiled pants and crying too.

John had no choice! He called his parents in North Carolina and asked if he could bring his family home to live on the farm. Fortunately, there was a small vacant house on the farm next to his older sister Betty & her husband Bright. His dad said that John could work for him at the Feed Co-Op store in town. John wrote a letter to the main office of Bonanza Airlines asking for an emergency leave of absence due to family medical problems. A week later, he traded the old yellow Model-A, for a dark green Chevrolet truck and they headed for North Carolina once more. His dad's farm was run down but at least it was a place to live and maybe Mott would be able to handle things better in familiar surroundings.

The small town of Plymouth was the County Seat yet it was located in a remote part of eastern North Carolina. The town originally founded by pirates, run away bond servants & outcasts in the 1700s, was located at the edge of The Great Dismal Swamp just 60 miles inland from the Atlantic Ocean on the Roanoke River. Politically, socially, and economically the Klan still ruled! Every business had separate entrances & service counters to keep the black people separated from the white folk. Tobacco was still the major source of income for the region along with corn & peanuts. It had the only indoor theatre in three counties.

State Highway 64 was a two-lane cement highway that ran through town and all the way to Cape Hatteras and the Atlantic

Ocean. There were only three stop signs in town, no streetlights, or stoplights. Mule drawn carts outnumbered cars on the road. Main street was just like it was when John & Mott had been children and gone to school in the 3-room wooden schoolhouse. The massive red brick high school down the street was the largest most modern building in town. Every city block in town had at least one marker dedicated to a civil war battle, always favoring Confederate victories. John's father, Vernis, was the County Veterinarian & Farm Agent. He was also the only "doctor" that would treat the black folk. Time and progress stood still in Plymouth.

Mott seemed to blossom in the familiar surroundings of Plymouth. She even played with Dane outside and decorated his bedroom. Often smiling while she did the housework, she felt happy once more. John was working long hours at the feed store and racing boats with his brother Jim on the Roanoke River once a month to keep his mind occupied. Jim and his wife Bert lived on the far side of the farm with their three kids. His sister Betty lived next door to John & Mott and had two children the same age. There were plenty of second cousins around too, so Dane was always around other kids. When Mott was not feeling well there was always someone available to take Dane for a few days or weeks.

John felt that perhaps everything would be okay now. If they could just pay off all of the doctor bills! There was not enough work and local wages were not high enough for John to attempt to save more than a couple of dollars each month. Maybe Mott was well enough for him to continue working for the airlines. John had never liked physical labor, he preferred to work inside, and there were not too many jobs like that around Plymouth. To obtain a better job would require them to move out west again and he didn't know how Mott would handle the stress. He absolutely did not want to be anywhere close to Cortez!

John wrote his old boss from Bonanza Airlines asking for his job back or any job position they would give him in January of 1953. Dane had started the first grade in the same little 3-room school house, with the same teacher that Mott had when she was in school.

He had to admit, the kid was showing some smarts. On the 15th of February a letter arrived from Bonanza Airlines. They were willing to take John back but he would have to work some isolated assignments for a while. The family had to move once more.

John & Mott packed all of their belongings into the back of the green Chevy pick-up. Mott's parents drove John downtown and picked Dane up at school. After a hushed discussion with his teacher, Mrs. Chessen, John told Dane that they had a surprise for him and that they had to go home. When they arrived at the little farm house, Mott was putting the last few little things in the truck. Her parents gave them all a tearful hug, got into their car, and drove off rapidly. John's parents dropped by within a few moments for a quick and tearful goodbye and then drove down the dirt road towards their farmhouse without looking back.

When Dane asked, what the surprise was, he was told, "We are moving out west." Mott hurriedly lifted him up into the cab of the truck, climbing in beside him. The Cocker Spaniel, Pepper was tucked between their legs on the floor of the truck. As they pulled out of the driveway, Dane's favorite kitten ran under the truck squealing as it was crushed by the rear tire. John did not stop or even slow down! He just told Dane "accidents happen"! As they drove down the highway the rusty poles of Dane's swing set rattled against the side of the truck. All of his favorite toys remained behind, as he had not even had a chance to go inside the house. His parents did not pack any of the toys, just the swing set.

CHAPTER ELEVEN

Jimmie-Kadena Air Force Base, Okinawa-1952

Mission completed and the B-29 was on the final approach to their base. During the flight, the radio was quiet because they were under orders for radio silence. It was easy to daydream on the way home if there were not too many problems. Occasionally, someone you knew was on a plane in trouble and going down within visual range. If they could break radio silence the pilot might send a cryptic message about the incident. You quickly learned to tune out some of the radio chatter. Knowing you would hear about every incident during the after action briefing upon their return. The crew would break their reverie as the plane neared home to talk about what they would do upon landing or when they could finally go home.

As the B-29 touched down on the runway, Jimmie saw the smoking shell of a bomber that had recently crashed on landing rushing past his plane. He cinched his harness tighter and tried to think of the breakfast he would have very shortly. Sometimes that was the best part of a mission! During the after-action briefing the pilot & bombardier described the combat action and all of the activity that had gone on up front. The anti-aircraft Flak, the mission's success or failure, and loss reports were always emotional topics. You quickly learned to ignore some things to avoid getting depressed.

A few members of the crew were talking about going into the tiny village tonight outside the base for a little celebrating or the Officers Club for drinks. Jimmie had mixed feelings about going with them, as he was not much for socializing. The village was small, mostly shacks, and what was considered "entertainment" didn't appeal to him. He had already watched the film showing in the base theater four times. Jimmie would probably stay in his tent, read a bit, maybe write a letter, and try to find a newspaper from stateside. Word had already come down the command chain that a big bombing run was coming up. It would be a difficult assignment. The mission would require a lot of preparation and extra work. Casualties could be high on this one!

Joan was at the Convent, preparing to take her Final Vows. She had chosen the name Sister Mary Jose. Writing the required good-by letters, burying the past and preparing to begin a new life. Her letter to Jimmie was the most difficult as he was going into combat and she was concerned that it might reach him during a difficult time. There was no choice in the matter! She had to send it to him now! Most of the letters had been easy to write. This was not easy and she was allowing her emotions to overrule her actions. She finally sought guidance from her Superior and spent several hours in prayer before she was able to finish the letter to Jimmie.

Jimmie received the letter from Joan three months after he arrived at Kadena, just as they were about to leave on another bombing mission. "Dearest Jimmie, you have been by heart & soul for so many years. The little brother that grew up so fast, now standing taller than your father did when he was alive. I am so proud of you for what you have accomplished in life. I am taking my Final Vows this week. You must understand, I have to leave the past behind and begin a new life in the Church. So you may not hear from me for a long time. I have to put away the memories and feelings of my past and cleanse my mind and Spirit in preparation for this new life. So for now my dear little brother, I am going to say good-by, may God Bless You, and keep you safe. I look forward to your safe return . . . Love you, Sis"

Jimmie reread the letter several times over the course of the afternoon. Each time a few more of his tears dropped onto the page. Finally, with a sigh, he folded it up very neatly and put it in his flight jacket pocket. Slowly walking towards their barracks tent, not really knowing what he wanted to do. Jimmie had only recently learned the gruesome details surrounding the Chosin Reservoir battle. The stories about what the soldiers had gone through and what Johnny Spruell must have suffered at Chosin were rather horrible. He had not heard about these things back home in Cortez! Adding in the emotions he felt about Johnnie's death and then receiving the letter from Joan made Jimmie feel angry, upset, and confused.

As Jimmie started up the path to the door of the tent, Fred Parker, the right gunner for their plane, came walking out and gave him a big smile. "Man you look like a mountain just fell on you! Let's go over the the Chapel. Maybe it'll get whatever is troubling you off of your back for a while." Jimmie absently minded nodded and fell into step with Fred. They slowly walked down the dusty street as Fred tried to cheer Jimmie up. Every so often Jimmie would put his hand up to the coat pocket just to make sure that letter was still there. Jimmie never heard from Joan again!

In a few days, the B-29 s of the 19th Bomb Group would be starting a new series of bombing missions, attacking the hydroelectric plants and rail systems. One big problem, the Russians & Chinese had brought in giant searchlights to use for their anti-aircraft guns. Now night bombing would not be so easy. They had to fly high enough to avoid the mountaintops yet low enough for the bombing to be effective so there was no place to hide. It was only the first week of September but the planes were constantly icing up over the mountain ranges. Any way you looked at it, the B-29s were like a flying icebox, always freezing inside. There were also new Russian MiGs that were good at night fighting; it was a very deadly combination of problems.

A letter from his older brother Richard arrives shortly before their next bombing mission started. His job is changing too. Richard has applied for a transfer into the Secret Service. Jimmie is interviewed a couple of days later for Richard's application by the Group Intelligence Officer about their family past and many personal questions about Richard. What if something happens to Richard too? They are the last of the family line! Now that Joan has gone into seclusion at the Convent, Jimmie was all alone. No family members were left that he can talk to or write letters! No girlfriends back home, no one to claim as his own. However, there is Mott & Dane! Jimmie writes her a letter that night, just hoping that she gets it and her husband does not see the letter.

Joan is in limbo at the Convent and can no longer communicate with anyone for an unknown amount of time. All he has left is his brother Richard, but he is now in a job where security is high and he cannot always write or receive letters. Jimmie and Richard were never close, as Richard was several years older and had left home when Jimmie was starting high school. He had never been much of a letter writer. That was just as bad as having no family at all! Mott is stuck in Arizona in a place she doesn't love with a man that yells and hits her. What is going to happen to little Dane? Jimmie goes through the daily routines while constantly thinking about his family and unable to resolve his feelings. He feels a dark shadow hanging over him and the future.

The next afternoon as the crews filed into the briefing tent to prepare for the big mission, Jimmie had a strange feeling that he would not be coming back from this trip. He made sure that all of his personal effects were in order and addressed one last letter to Joan, telling her about Mott and Dane. She needed to know that he had a son! The Air Force would notify Mott and his two siblings if anything happened to Jimmie. Why did this mission bother him so much? At 4pm all the crews filed into the briefing tent to receive the latest updates prior to departing. Jimmie quietly uttered a prayer as he sat down and the Executive Officer began to speak.

BOMBING RUN—SUIHO DAM 13 SEP 52

The squadron was ready! Bombs were loaded, everyone had been busy during the day preparing the aircraft, cleaning weapons, making adjustments and checking their personal equipment. All of the air crews began to assemble in the briefing tent for final instructions. A new flight crew had arrived; their captain would have to fly one mission with a seasoned crew to learn local procedures. The Commander assigned Captain Lowe to fly Jimmie's B-29, instead of Captain Howell who they had trained with since flight school at Randolph Field.

Tonight was the night they targeted the fourth largest power plant & dam in the world at Suiho, near the Manchurian border. It was going to be a rough mission because of all the radar-controlled searchlights recently installed around the dam. The power plant was also close to an airfield staffed with Russian MiG-15 fighters. There were 300 heavy anti-aircraft gun emplacements on the mountaintops around the area, able to cover every square inch of the sky. A well-trained Russian Artillery Regiment operated both the searchlights and the gun emplacements. Jimmie had a real bad feeling about the mission. It wasn't going to be an easy night!

Earlier in the day, Jimmie had cleaned his guns, checked the ammunition and all of his gear several times. Each crewmember helped the others double check and prepare their equipment. They had been working on the aircraft all day with only a few short breaks. Everyone sensed this was going to be a tough mission. Jimmie walked around the airfield during one of their few breaks, reading Joan's letter again and thinking about what her life would be like in a Convent. Glancing at the 'Bombs Loaded' sign by the nose wheel

Jimmie stood under the wing of his plane, watching the changing colors in the clouds as the sun sank into the ocean. A cold wind was blowing from the north, with a shiver he zipped up his leather flight jacket.

It was time to load up. The pilot inspected the crew with all of their gear spread out in front of the bomber, making sure everything was in order. Easing his six foot four frame into the life vest & parachute, Jimmie climbed the metal ladder up into the fuselage and took his stand-by position by the Auxiliary Power Unit. The propellers were turned. Last minute checks to make sure his area was secured. During the flight he would be isolated from rest of the crew.

The engines start one by one with a cough. Exhaust smoke billows past his viewport. Brakes release and the heavily loaded bomber lumbered toward the taxi strip for takeoff. Engines revved with more safety checks made. Suddenly, with a lurch the overloaded bomber sluggishly begins to move. As they gain speed Jimmie looks out the small Plexiglas window. The ground rushes by faster & faster. He sees members of the ground crew waving as they lift off the ground. There is that strange feeling in the pit of his stomach again. Would they make it back from this mission?

The crew is unusually quiet as the bomb laden B-29 reaches cruising altitude at 24,000 feet and the pilot sets the course for Suiho. The bombers passed the Korean coastline heading inland in their usual single file stream. The radio channel between the planes was silent. As a precaution, the crew tried not to use the on-board com channel in case it could be picked up by the enemy. Jimmie ponders about Joan's life at the Convent and Richard in his new job with the Secret Service. Will I ever see them again? When will Mott receive his last letter? Jimmie had asked her to send him a picture of Dane.

Around midnight the navigator radios that the target is coming up. Jimmie tried to warm his fingers up. Even with the fur lined gloves on they were cold. Double checks his gun and ammo absentmindedly. The Radar Observer began to give course corrections to the Aircraft

Commander as they approached the target. The order was passed down to depressurize the plane so that the bulkhead hatches could be opened quickly in the case of an emergency. Suddenly searchlights focus directly on their B-29 as the bomb bay doors open.

CHAPTER TWELVE

DANE—REFLECTIONS OF THE PAST

I stayed away from mother & father for a couple of years after graduating from high school. Yet out of a sense of guilt that everything was my fault, I tried to reconnect with them several times. However my parents made it quite clear each time that I wasn't part of the family and they didn't want me around anymore. When I did call or visit, mother would usually end up having a tantrum, claiming I did not love her and that I was doing all sorts of things to hurt her. Father just acted as if I was a neighbor, dropping by for a chat. Most of the time, he would ignore me after a few minutes and fall asleep in his recliner or busy himself outside. Always avoiding conversation unless I forced the situation, then his replies would be very short. I felt like a stranger in their home!

Mother became more obsessed with her faith healing, spending most of the day in "meditation," yet her medical problems increased. The Christian Science Church had excommunicated her in 1972 because of her self-prescribed combination of medications & spiritualism plus her many hospitalizations. Sadly mother would claim the Christian Science Church membership when she didn't want to follow doctor's orders.

Dad built a custom home in north Phoenix, surrounded by an eight-foot brick wall. It became mother's sanctuary for the next twenty years and the only time she went outside the walls was for doctor's appointments or an infrequent trip in the small vacation trailer he had bought. John could leave Mott all day in that house while he was at work. If she needed anything he would take care of it when he returned. John had left the airline industry and formed a construction company with two other business partners, specializing in office plazas. That business failed due to his refusal to work with his business partners. Things were done his way or not at all!

For a couple of years in the 1980s they "adopted" kids in the neighborhood and began taking them on trips, doing things with them that they had never done with me. I had finally understood many years before that my mother had a "fascination" for very young men. Especially those post-adolescent boys in their teens! Sometimes I wondered if she had other motives because of the parade of young men throughout her life!

One young man, their paperboy for several years, became a favorite. His name was Ray, very intelligent, athletic, and talented. When his parents had arguments, he would stay with my parents. Later, when Ray was old enough, my parents bought him his first car. They even gave him a bedroom to stay in, so he would not have to change schools when his parents moved away to another town. Part of his college tuition was paid by them! My parents took care of Ray, as they had never done for me! When Ray started getting into trouble with the police because of drug problems and credit card theft, they acted as though he was innocent. Even after he was convicted and did six months in jail! As time passed, even Ray could not coerce mother to leave the house except once or twice a year. John continued to work at a variety of jobs and investing in ventures that promised easy money but they always seemed to fail for some reason.

Dropping by their house as a courtesy the week I joined the Army to say good-by. Father said the military was a waste of time and asked why I didn't get a more "respectable job." Periodically over the next ten years, I made contact with them without any improvement or success in our relationship. Finally, I gave up trying to be part of their family and began counseling through the Army to resolve some of the emotional issues that plagued me. Our family differences were never resolved! When I was injured and retired from the army the Veteran's Administration appointed my father as temporary guardian since he was my closest living relative. Our relationship status never changed! He went through the motions dutifully, frequently making it quite clear that he considered the task an imposition. Father really didn't want to be 'bothered' with my situation.

He sold their house in north Phoenix in 1993 for $25,000 cash. I could have easily bought the home and had comfortable place to live for the rest of my life. It was valued in those days at over two hundred thousand dollars! Cramming as much of their possessions as possible into a 24 foot U-Haul truck. He gave away the remainder without offering any of it to me. Two days after selling the house he put mother in the rental moving truck with her two Schipperke dogs and drove back to their hometown in North Carolina. Father bought a double wide trailer which they lived in for six months then bought a brick home that was falling apart. Thirty days later they had to move back into the trailer as the brick house was in such bad shape. Father died a few months later in April of 1995 of a brain tumor, cursing me loudly on his death bed when his sister asked if I could visit.

Mother had become a total recluse in their home in Phoenix and continued the same behavior when they moved back to Carolina. She would hobble around the back yard and feed the birds or water her flowers but would refuse to leave the property, always finding an excuse even though her brother & sister lived right down the street. She insisted that she could not leave the house except to go to the doctor. Mother spent each day in meditation, reading scripture or napping on the couch with the TV blaring loudly.

Preferring to pay someone to do even the simplest household chore rather than do it herself. The life insurance money from her husband's death was frivolously spent. Within a short time she hired a young black man named Larry to cook, clean house & keep the yard mowed. He was mentally a bit slow and had a prison record and for a while he kept her home spotless. Over the next couple of years she bought him a car, a pickup truck, clothes, and paid some of his bills. Family members would offer to help or do something for her and she would tell them that she trusted Larry more than she trusted them.

That statement caused considerable problems within the family and tension in the neighborhood. Their fears were well founded because two years later it was discovered he had emptied mother's storage locker full of furniture and household goods and sold all of the items. In addition, he had convinced her to pay him over five thousand dollars for non-existent expenses. Within five years she had wasted over 250 thousand dollars from the insurance annuity. That money was intended to supplement her Social Security & Medicare, helping to cover her expenses for the rest of her life.

Mother created her own religion, as the churches that she had been associated with in the past did not condone her unusual beliefs. Especially the Christian Science Church! She began to self-medicate, even using old medicines that had belonged to other people and claiming, "A doctor had told her it was okay." The schizophrenia was now in control of Mother's life and the family members in North Carolina didn't understand that she needed medical & mental health care so they just left her alone as much as possible. Their attempts to help her were often rebuffed by temper tantrums and baseless accusations.

In retrospect, looking back on my life now, I wonder how I had managed to break out of the mold and join the army! Strangely, the army had been my saving grace, and it had given me a new life. The first job was working as a Personnel Clerk and it became apparent that I had a knack for detailed paperwork though my "people skills" needed a lot of work and improvement. Fortunately as time passed I was able to pick up several leadership & management courses. Cross training in several different career fields over the years made life in the military easier. I was always in demand in some position or another. Over one ten year period I was actually assigned to several different headquarters commands performing a variety of duties in other locations. The military called that type of an assignment a TDY or Temporary Duty or Attached Duty. Some of the jobs were challenging, some were fun, and others required long hard hours of dangerous work.

Working in the Military Intelligence field, as an analyst was a challenge and quite fulfilling as an occupation. However, the 18 months I spent in Germany assigned to a non-existent position at the Mannheim Regional Personnel Center while I infiltrated a local Neo Nazi organization was possibly the most difficult task of my life. I kept that assignment a secret for over thirty years for fear of retribution from the Germans involved in the organization. Several "Odessa" type organizations continue to provide assistance & money to former Nazi leaders and their extended families. Many of the organizations had extensive contacts and members living in the United States and other countries and some are still active today.

Though the assignment as a Judge Advocate Team Inspector at Fort Sam Houston was daunting at times, I was often required to make decisions that could make or break an officer or enlisted man's career. I guess you could call me a "company man" as I detested corruption, prejudice, or the mistreatment of soldiers. Yes, even the military has those problems!

While working at Ft. Sam Houston in 1986 I began doing volunteer work for several of the local aid & hospice agencies in San Antonio. That was when the AIDS epidemic was first attracting public attention. Unfortunately there was very little accurate information available to the public or the medical profession. Lackland Air Force Base Hospital near San Antonio was chosen to manage a joint-service hospital ward for men identified as having

HIV/AIDS. Sadly, the military stance at that time was if a man contracted HIV then he must be a homosexual. Therefore he was given a less than honorable discharge without further medical care. If he lived that long!

It didn't matter to the military if the man contracted HIV through blood transfusion, prostitutes, drug use, from his spouse, or any other method. Soldiers were quarantined in small rooms with limited human contact, told they were about to die, possibly before their discharge papers could be completed. This cold hearted response caused several men to just give up and die within thirty days of their arrival in the ward!

The pastor of my church, aware of my training and volunteer work, asked if I would assist him by participating as a "lay preacher" during my off-duty hours. After meeting with one of the officers in charge of the program, I was allowed to go into the hospital rooms at Lackland AFB, talk with the men, and pray with them. During the six months I did this volunteer work the pastor & I met several times with various doctors and officers at the hospital. Over time the medical staff received additional training and new information regarding HIV/AIDS; it was no longer a "gay" disease. The hospital ward became a pilot program for handling military personnel with HIV in a compassionate manner.

Some of the assignments I left behind with commanders & supervisors that didn't like me because I stuck to the Regulations and fought for the rights of the lower ranking soldiers. Yet from others I received high praise from the officers in charge because of my reliability and dedication. Overall, integrity and a high level of work performance led to several fast promotions and many commendations as my career progressed.

No matter how hard I tried, there were still some hidden demons rattling around in my head and I could not ask for counseling or guidance from the army due to the nature of some of the military assignments and a high security clearance. Often I utilized my off-duty volunteer work as a way to obtain, private counseling, or assistance. If I had asked for help, my commanders would have immediately transferred me to another job or even kicked me out of the army. The only solution was to keep quiet and suffer through some long dark nights!

Alcohol became a solution for many years, as drugs would have instantly been cause for discharge. The military had no problem in looking the other way when it came to their senior staff over indulging in alcohol. As long as you got the job done! Some commanders actually required senior staff to drink during meetings or activities. Alcohol was a requirement for promotions, retirements, and other military functions. The excessive drinking destroyed a marriage to a wonderful woman and several relationships so I finally decided that it was safer not to get involved in long term affairs. A single life was less complicated, though very lonely at times.

When I became stale in a job I quickly learned how to wangle a transfer into another position or assignment. Often leaning on friendships and playing "dirty" politics. Sometimes that was a way to escape emotional attachments or because I did not get along with my commander. Still, I had a good reputation and as time progressed, I found myself listed in the top five percent of the army's enlisted leadership and classed as an expert in several fields by the end of my eighteenth year of service. The army had provided the chance for travel & adventure that I could never have achieved on my own. It also paid for two college degrees and continued to send me to additional military and civilian schools to maintain my proficiency.

Requesting special or difficult assignments just for the challenge and a change of pace was also a rationalized escape mechanism. Most of the time I was successful and then there were times when I fell flat on my face. I would have to do some fancy foot work to get out of the situation. I had no real family, no one to be concerned about me so being a professional soldier was easy. Keeping an updated Will and making sure that my ever-growing collection of memorabilia would be properly dispersed according to my wishes after I died seemed easy. Looking back now, I realize that I often courted death or expected to die young so I didn't plan for or even look to the future. My life and chosen career was the army. Long ago I had accepted and welcomed the fact that my life in the military was expendable.

Occasionally, those old hidden demons would crawl out of their holes, playing havoc with my life. Several times over the years despite previous failures, I did try to reconnect with my parents, always to no avail. Regardless of the counselors telling me it was a bad idea. I still hungered for reconciliation and family connections. Mother could be so loving one moment and then yelling and cursing the next. Father just treated me as if I was a stranger passing by, never interested in my life or me as an individual. We seemed to live in separate universes!

Once in a while something would occur that would make my father seem almost human! One day I had gone into Phoenix to pick up something for a friend and was standing at the counter waiting for them to bring a box to me. Suddenly a woman sitting at a desk behind the counter jumps up. She runs around the counter towards me yelling my name, grabs me in her arms, and gives me a big hug. It had been almost fifteen years but I recognized June right away. She had been father's private secretary when he was the Bonanza Airlines Station Manager at the Phoenix airport for several years while I was in high school.

I had been required to call his office each day to let him know when I got home from school. She was the one notified when I would get into trouble instead of my mother. June & father had an affair that lasted for several years, which I knew about. I had often heard her name mentioned when my parents would have an argument. June's petite 5'4" stature had gained quite a few pounds and her hair now had streaks of grey. Yet her bright blue eyes still sparkled, especially when she smiled. We talked for a few minutes about our lives and June said that she still loved my father. When I left her office that day Joan gave me a tearful hug and was still crying as I drove off.

About a year later, I saw my father on one of the construction sites he was managing near Fort Huachuca in southern Arizona.

Stopping to pass the time as a courtesy but still expecting the usual cold shoulder. During the course of conversation I mentioned that I had run into June. Pausing in mid-sentence, he sat down on a stack of cinder blocks and said, "June was a fine woman, she was in love with me." After a few moments of silence, he quietly asked about what we had talked about and how she looked after all these years. While we talked, he just kept staring out across the desert landscape and digging in the sand with the toe of his boot. That was the first time my father had ever shown any real emotion! The man never did understand that I knew about several of his affairs and that one of the women had even made a pass at me while she was still seeing him when I was working at the airport before I joined the army.

Volunteering for recruiting duty was a crazy idea though it did get me away from San Antonio and my ex-wife. I had a personal code of ethics that I always followed and found it difficult to compromise those ethics just because a Commander said so. I truly felt that code of ethics would do me good on recruiting duty. As it turned out I was a good military recruiter! I didn't lie to the kids or try to steal the prospects from other recruiters and was always honest in trying to convince them to join the Army. The first recruiting assignment was for a year covering the inner city projects of Dallas, Texas. I was the only white recruiter in a ten-man station and the only recruiter in the station that would drive into the projects to meet prospective applicants.

That annoying code of ethics didn't allow me to lie or pressure the applicants much to the displeasure of a few of my fellow recruiters. It took me a couple of months to get started but once again, I was an over achiever in the job. As a result, when other recruiters failed to make their monthly quota I had to work mandatory overtime to make up for their failures. Consistent success allowed me to eventually transfer to another station that covered the rural communities south of Dallas.

Unfortunately, the recruiting mission quota for that region was being drastically increased due to overseas commitments by the American military and the beginning of Desert Shield/Desert Storm. The number of kids willing to join was rapidly decreasing so we began spending twelve to sixteen hour workdays trying to meet the quotas. I still managed to line up kids for the future and meet my quota each month. However, it became obvious that the physical and mental strain on the recruiters working six & seven days a week for that many hours could have disastrous results. The regional recruiting command had enjoyed over 56 consecutive months of exceeding or meeting the mandated recruiting quota for the Army Reserves and most of the time for the Regular Army. However, that record was shattered by the sudden drop caused by Desert Storm. To this day, I consider my recruiting photo to be the best one ever taken of me while I was in uniform.

CHAPTER THIRTEEN

-DANE-2008-THE SEARCH CONTINUES-

I have been searching now for months, trying to find out more information on Airman First Class Jimmie Hobday. It was very frustrating, as I wasn't having very much luck with the veterans groups and their websites or in finding anything out about his personal or family life. The veteran's reunion groups from the Korean War had been disappointing in their limited response. The tedious searching of government archive records online could be exasperating if not impossible at times.

Then at the end of August 2008, I had an email from Frank 'Bud' Farrell that changed everything! I had placed a request in the 307th Bomb Wing Quarterly Newsletter, asking if anyone had knowledge or information about the crew or the bomber that went down over Suiho Dam in Korea September 1952. Mr. Farrell asked for my phone number and said he wanted to talk. 'Bud' Farrell called that night and we spent a couple of tearful hours on the phone and at least a hundred emails over the next couple of days. He was in the B-29 bomber behind Jimmie's when it exploded in mid-air over

Suiho. His subsequent phone call provided a prodigious amount of information and the start of a very special friendship. A few days after our initial phone conversation 'Bud' sent me an excerpt from his book "No Sweat," that told the story of Jimmie's B-29 from an entirely different perspective. Reading the excerpt for the first time, I was crying before I had even finished reading the first page.

"As tired as we all were after the mission, physically and mentally exhausted. Nearly everyone in the squadron and group wanted to be on the flight line early the next day to look at aircraft damage and to await crews returning from emergency landings at bases in South Korea or Japan for repair or refueling . . . Throughout the day numerous aircraft started drifting back into Kadena, filling empty slots on hard stands along miles of taxiway ramps of the 19ᵗʰ and 307ᵗʰ And up the hill terraced by ramps & hard stands, at the 307ᵗʰ Bomb Wing area, there was another open hard stand that would not be filled for a while . . . the ship that blew up in front of us. A week after Suiho, I found out that a friend of mine from gunnery school, Fred Parker, was on that ship and I had seen him no more than a week before in the PX and he was very excited about completing his combat tour in a few weeks and returning home to his wife and a brand new baby boy born just two weeks earlier.

At the Suiho debriefing our Crew reported in good faith that we did not believe that anyone had or could have survived the explosion of the B-29 in front of us, but it was dark, midnight, and impossible to have seen chutes or anything other than the falling burning wreckage. For one year, until August 1953, I thought about Fred and scanned all of the newspaper POW repatriation lists after the July 27ᵗʰ 1953 Truce ending the war . . . and there was Fred Parker! Thank God!"

Reading that chapter in "No Sweat" gave me goose bumps! The B-29 that exploded over Suiho Dam was the plane and crew that Jimmie Hobday was assigned to and flying on that dreadful night in 1952. No one had thought there could possibly be any survivors with the resulting fireball yet somehow Fred Parker had survived! Another person was possibly still alive that had known Jimmie!

Would I ever be able to talk with him after all these years? Would he know anything about Jimmie and my mother?

Frank Farrell, 'Bud' to his friends, and I emailed and talked by phone for several days. I wrote him a letter and included a copy of the two page story that I had written and various photos. The next thing I know, he sent me an email, with the 'draft' of a chapter he wanted to add to the upcoming Revised Edition of his book "No Sweat." It was very flattering, and an odd feeling, seeing your own life story in print, written by someone else.

"Our nation honors her sons and daughters who answered a call to defend a country they never knew and a people they never met." . . . Korean War Memorial—

Paraphrasing that, Dane's father, Jimmie Hobday, answered a call to defend a country he never knew and a people he never met . . . with a son he had by a love he never kept . . . Dane now had a father & mother who were never again to be together and yet never to be forgotten . . . unlike "The Forgotten War", Korea, that kept them all apart!" . . . Bud Farrell.

Bud knew someone in the Pentagon, Phil O'Brien, who worked in the POW Division. He felt this man should know where Fred Parker was living and would be able to assist me in contacting Fred. I called Phil the next day and he provided me with a phone number and address for Fred, warning me that Fred was in poor health. Fred didn't like to discuss his days as a POW and probably would not spend much time on the phone. A few days later, I finally got the nerve up to call Fred, who was now living on a farm in southern Arkansas.

Again, it was a tearful phone call! Contrary to Phil's prediction, Fred was eager to talk once I explained who I was and why I had called him. I promised to write and send him some information. He thought there might be a couple of other men that were still around that knew Jimmie but he wasn't sure if he had their correct addresses. Fred said he would send me his remembrances of Jimmie and see if he could contact the others to do the same. The experience as a POW in Korea at Prison Camp #2 so traumatized Fred that he was never the same after the war. He just wouldn't talk about it to anyone! The memories of the ordeal had haunted Fred all of his life and he shied away from anyone that asked him about his experience in the war. Yet during that phone call he shared a few things with me! However he didn't send me a package! A few weeks later I sent Fred another letter with no response.

Bud Farrell wrote him a letter also without any response either. Then the last week of October, I tried once more, only to have a bad phone connection and Fred couldn't hear me. I gave up! Then to my surprise, the next evening he called me back. Fred told me that he has been suffering from a severe case of pneumonia. He was still trying to bring his crops in on his small farm before the winter snows arrive. Apologizing twice for not getting back to me and said he was putting a packet in the mail this week, with several photos. That he would try to answer all the questions in my letter to the best of his memory about Jimmie and Korea.

Fred and I talked about Jimmie and a few of the things that had happened since we last spoke. Jimmie's sister, Sister Jose, had never called him after I told her that Fred Parker was still alive. Considering her isolation within the Tucson Convent and illness, it was not really expected. We discussed the pending Memorial Ceremony for Jimmie at Arlington National Cemetery. Fred felt that between his health and being short of money, he couldn't make it to the Ceremony, but he did ask me to send him some pictures. He sounded happy and glad to talk with me about Jimmie and the war.

Later I called Bud Farrell and told him about the phone call and he urged me again to write a book about my life and all the things that had happened. I didn't think Fred Parker would live much longer based on the way he sounded and the medical problems he described. Several months later Bud Farrell relayed a recent telephone conversation with Fred Parker. Apparently, Fred had recovered from his illness and his health was much better. Perhaps we would still have a chance to meet someday! Bud lamented that he hadn't been in the position to go see Fred after all these years, perhaps someday in the future.

The second week of November in 2008, a letter arrived from Sister Jose. The Air Force Casualty Office had recently sent her an official display set of the medals awarded to Jimmie. In the letter, she said, "It is difficult for me to look at them, Dane. Such small substitutes for a life, yes?" In our next telephone conversation, Sister Jose mentions that she may give the medals away as they bring back too many memories. Had she grown that unemotional about her life? We turned our discussion to her books and lectures that I had been reading. I found Sister Jose's philosophy comforting and told her that I was surprised at her wealth of knowledge on current social attitudes. She said with a chuckle, "I may be a Nun, but that is no reason for me to keep my head stuck in the sand." Even at my age and jaded past, Sister Jose felt that she could teach me a few things about life!

Because of Sister Jose's poor vision and her many medical issues, it was easier for us to have long telephone conversations instead of writing letters. I shared with her some of the childhood and adult issues that I had worked on during the years of intense counseling. Quite often, the depth of Sister Jose's knowledge and understanding surprised me along with some of her suggestions and answers. She had a profound knowledge of family dynamics & abuse issues so her comments were often exacting and very direct. She must have been a great counselor and public speaker!

Unfortunately, our discussions became shorter as her illness rapidly progressed and the frequency of her phone calls lessened. Gaining a dear friend and confidant only to find that we wouldn't have much time to know each other was in itself frustrating. Both of us felt a 'connection' even though I held back talking about our possible relationship. Sometimes in our discussions I sensed that though she had immersed herself into the lives of others and the happenings around the world, she felt more like an observer than a participant. However, in the course of our many discussions I perceived that Sister Jose knew more about my situation than she let on. That lady was one smart cookie!

CHAPTER FORTEEN

Dane—In Harm's Way—October 1989

For several years after I retired from the Army, I was embarrassed or afraid to talk about the injuries that had done so much damage to my body. I even created a more 'adventurous' scenario so that folks wouldn't ask too many questions. As time went along and I met folks that came to know me and my background they reassured me that no one would think less of me because of the un-heroic circumstances. After all the different things that had been accomplished in my life, my military career, all of the dangerous situations that I had been in, it just seemed so anti-climactic and unfair! I had survived parachute jumps into dangerous places, broken & fractured bones, covert assignments, and even death threats. Only to be brought down by an odd twist of fate! Bud Farrell & Frank Nagy also urged me to be truthful about the situation.

Highly successful in my military profession, an over achiever in several different fields, life had been good despite everything that had happened to me. My military career had been very enjoyable and rewarding. I had traveled the world, obtained two college degrees, and felt that I had led a good life. Performing as a recruiter without having to resort to lies or tricks seemed to be icing on the cake. Barely one year after becoming a recruiter, assigned to one of the largest areas in Texas and rising again to the top of my field in a short time!

Unfortunately, that all came to an abrupt end one day six months after I had transferred from inner city Dallas to the suburbs! I was at the local military processing center in Dallas one morning walking through the parking lot. When a man called me over to his car, and then all I remembered after that was a dark skinned arm grabbing me and placing something over my head. I was mugged right in a government parking lot in downtown Dallas! Their deliberate attempt to murder and rob me must have been interrupted. Even though I was robbed and left nearly dead, they didn't kill me.

However, the damage done inside my body was severe; I should have died from the concussion and suffocation. A blood clot had formed in my brain. At first, it just affected short-term memory and then over time it continued to shift position causing more problems and damage. The police found me three days later, wandering the back streets; I didn't know who I was or what had happened. After a few days in a Fort Worth hospital with no in-depth exams. Rather than have me examined further at a military hospital he sent me home with instructions to return to duty the next day.

Within a couple of days it was obvious that I was having problems, my commander then ordered me to take two weeks Leave and rest. Upon returning to duty I couldn't function very well and so my Commander had me sent to Fort Hood Military Hospital in northern Texas for further evaluation. He believed I was either faking the problems, had been drunk, or had just gone nuts! I was slowly losing the feeling and control in my arms & legs and experiencing extreme pain along with transient memory problems even though my body had not shown any signs of severe trauma on the outside. Sometime later, I woke up in the ICU at Fort Hood Hospital. They had almost lost me a couple of times. The doctors constantly ran tests every week to see if I made any improvements. Instead, additional problems kept appearing which they could not explain!

I had a severe permanent migraine headache and wasn't able to adequately control my arms & legs. There were giant gaps in my long-term memory and my short-term memory was so messed up that as each day ended the present and the past began to have large empty spaces. My eyes kept blurring out which made it difficult to read, and I couldn't talk clearly. It felt was as though I was swimming through Jell-O physically and mentally. When I tried to talk, at times people could not understand what I was saying so I would become very frustrated and angry.

Medication dosages were increased to dangerously high levels in an attempt to stop the permanent migraine headache, muscle spasms & constant body pain. Sometimes the high dose of medications worked, and then sometimes it didn't, usually resulting in another trip to the emergency room. My body would shut down or reject the large doses of medications causing even more problems. Life had become extremely painful and frustrating.

After several weeks, I was getting to the point where I could slowly talk and the nursing staff could understand me. Fortunately I had a fine group of doctors (mostly Army Reservists) that felt I was worth saving rather than just shipping me off to a nursing home. The regular active duty staff doctors from Ft. Hood had been sent overseas because of Desert Shield & Desert Storm so these doctors & nurses were civilian professionals. Part time warriors brought on active duty and assigned to temporarily staff the hospital. These people really cared about the person, not just body count! I now believe that made the difference between my living and dying.

One day, I finally realized and accepted the fact that my life, as I knew it was over and spent all day crying. The nurses just brought in a couple of boxes of tissues, set the trash can next to the bed and closed the door. Thankfully I had a private room! After a couple of hours, a doctor came into the room and said, "We have been waiting for this, now we can begin trying to heal you, if you are willing. It will not be easy, it will not be without lots of pain and frustration. However if you will try, we will do all that we can before we are required to send your file to a Medical Board for Retirement."

For several months, we worked every day. Physical therapy, speech therapy, testing, counseling, and so many other things I couldn't remember them. I was able to talk, slowly at first, but at least I was talking and starting to think clearly if I was not rushed. Still, there was no clear memory of the past and even what had went on just a few days, sometimes hours before. I had short-term memory problems and had to learn how to cope with that and the inability to do the everyday things I had done all of my life. It was still difficult to express myself, my brain worked but I could not speak clearly or in complete sentences. This made communication difficult and some folks then assumed I was mentally incompetent.

Finally, through medical, newspaper, and police reports the hospital staff helped me piece together what had happened. A nurse typed out the information and insisted that I read it every day so that I would not forget. I had fallen victim to a group of men that were going around in a van kidnapping and robbing people. They had killed several of their victims and their favorite way of capturing or disabling their intended victim was to come up from behind, using a plastic bag to suffocate the person.

Their attempt to suffocate me or kill me had caused severe brain/body damage yet I somehow survived, possibly because I had been in such good physical shape. The local newspaper, The Dallas Morning News, had run an article about the robbers being captured a few months after I was injured and in the hospital. There are still many unanswered questions about this event and no way to know exactly why and how everything happened. I do know that the police found me wandering incoherently about 10 miles away from my duty station dressed in rags. A few days later, the police later found my empty wallet by the side of a freeway twenty miles away on the other side of town.

The Fort Hood medical staff did everything possible to help me improve, quite often stretching the military regulations to the limit. If it had been peace time the regular military doctors would have processed me for retirement without trying to help me salvage my life. The Army Reserve doctors and nurses, the weekend warriors, were trying to help me recover and get to the point where I could function on my own. I am very grateful for their efforts as I realize now that they went far beyond what was required by medical/military regulations! Their efforts will always be remembered.

One morning a doctor came in to the hospital room, placing a wheelchair near the bed as he talked. He said that they had a choice, they could retire me directly to a Veterans Nursing Home for the rest of my life, since I was bed bound and could not get into a wheelchair without assistance. Or I could crawl out of that bed, get into a wheelchair, and no matter how much it hurt, move myself around the hospital and continue treatment. The doctor said he wanted me to think about it overnight and he would be back in the morning to talk before he made a final decision. He turned and walked out of the room, never really saying a word about the wheelchair he had placed a few feet from my bed. During the course of the day the nurses totally ignored the wheelchair when they came into the room.

That was a rough night! Somehow, I managed to roll off the edge of the bed, crawl over to the wheelchair, and pull myself up into the chair. Trying to move felt as if I was moving through thick mud and I was totally worn out by the exertion! When that doctor came back the next morning I was still sitting in the wheelchair. I was afraid that if I tried to get back into the hospital bed I would fall flat on my face. Then I would be stuck on the floor for the rest of the night. The doctor smiled and said he had expected to see me in the chair, as he did not believe that I would quit very easily. All I could think of at that moment was getting to the bathroom so I could pee! To this day, no matter how hard I try, I cannot remember his name! Someday I would like to shake his hand and thank him. We started to work that day on creating a new life for me, at times it hurt so bad I cried and prayed for it to end. I kept going!

After ten months in that Fort Hood hospital room the military doctors decided that they could do no more and began processing my file to be submitted to the Retirement Board and mandatory medical retirement. I was on heavy medications for pain and panic attacks. The left side of my body was numb and did not work right. Both legs had severe periodic muscle spasms that would bring tears to my eyes. I had double vision and a permanent migraine type headache. A small TENS unit, with electrodes attached to my neck each morning, provided temporary relief from the migraine headache. I had to wear the TENS unit at least twelve hours a day. My speech was still slow and slurred. There were short term and long term memory deficits with gaps in memories from my earlier years. At least I was alive!

The daily visits to physical therapy and counseling continued right up to the last week prior to my retirement three weeks later. I had been allowed to leave the hospital for Christmas to stay with friends in Fort Worth. That proved to be a disaster! They did not feel comfortable around me so I was left alone much of the time. The army had contacted my parents since I was legally incapacitated, assigning my father as guardian, which really scared the hell out of me. He flew in from Phoenix one weekend to see me and made it very clear that he would "see me settled" but did not have a lot of time to spend "taking care of me."

My personal belongings and furniture crammed into the mobile home I had rented in a trailer park between Dallas and Fort Worth were packed up. I returned to Phoenix mid-April of 1991. Father set me up in an economy apartment, built sometime in the early 1950s in north Phoenix. Dust billowed up from the old mottled green shag carpet no matter how often it was vacuumed. The apartment was not close to a city bus line and there were no stores in the area so he grudgingly brought my groceries and mail to me a couple of times each week. All I could do was sit and look out the window. There had been more freedom in the hospital room!

The weather was shifting from spring to summer in Phoenix. The days were rapidly becoming warmer even though it was still storming up in the mountains of northern Arizona. That apartment became very hot and stuffy despite the air conditioner. Six months of sitting in that wheelchair, looking out the living room window of that cloister like apartment brought things into clarity. If I was going to live I needed to change things and soon! Vegetating in that chair was worse than death!

However, a milestone occurred during that period I will never forget. I had framed all of my military awards & letters of commendation and placed them on one entire wall of the bedroom. When my father brought over groceries one day he looked at the wall for about five minutes, turned to me saying, "Well I guess you did something in your life!" That was the highest compliment he had ever given me!

Each visit by him was the same. He would walk into the kitchen, place a box of groceries on the table, ask if I was okay, and then walk out. As the days passed, my body began to get used to the heavy pain medications that the Veteran's Hospital had issued to me. No longer sleeping half the day and walking around in a drug induced stupor, I finally started to feel human again.

Each day stretched into a set routine. I would wake up, take meds and eat breakfast. After I showered & shaved the day would be spent looking out the window or watching TV unless I had to go the VA hospital. Sometimes I would spend hours going through two large cardboard boxes of leather crafts & small projects which I kept in the living room next to a folding table. The physical therapist from Fort Hood said they would help my coordination & thinking processes. After a while they became boring. Then one day I looked at several of my finished items, realizing the crafts had indeed helped me during my recovery but they were all useless items. Why was I saving them?

The VA had a two-year backlog in processing disability claims during that period so the interim care was not the best. Much needed physical therapy & counseling were skipped because my file was still listed as "temporary." I not only had to do copay on my prescriptions, but also had to sit sometimes for six to eight hours just waiting to see a doctor. As a result I would sometimes spend every day of the week sitting in one of the hospital clinics waiting to be seen. Once my file was processed medical care would be free and I would have regular scheduled appointments.

I came to realize that if I stayed in that apartment I would probably end up killing myself! One day I gathered up enough strength to wheel down to the little corner store and buy a Phoenix newspaper. The classified ads had many rooms & apartments available that were cheaper than the dump father had found for me. Over the next few weeks, a systematic search was made trying to find a new place to live. The main goal was to be centrally located so I could do shopping, a short distance from the VA Hospital and have public transportation access too. The City Transit service did offer a discounted bus pass for disabled persons which I quickly applied for and received within just a few days.

By the end of October, I had found a new home about four miles away in downtown Phoenix. A three-bedroom house for rent at the very same price as the little apartment and it was near the Veteran's hospital too! It was an older home that had been remodeled and was situated on a corner lot. It had wheelchair access through the front door and a large shaded back porch where I could sit. The neighborhood was not the best but the location made up for any potential problems. My father did not like the idea of me moving but when I explained that he would no longer have to bring groceries or give me rides to the doctor he was very happy and offered no further objections. However, he would be too busy to help me move!

I planned to advertise for a roommate or two to save on money and they would be able to help me around the house too. Packing up my stuff was easy and a friend had a truck that we used to move furniture and clothes. Once moved into the new house, my parents visited me only twice over the next six months. Each visit was short, as they always seemed to be in a rush to leave as soon as possible. The move into the house also began a renewal of life. Regaining some strength and finding that I could walk a short distance with the aid of a cane or walker allowed me to go out in public again.

Occasionally I would use the wheelchair downtown but that was difficult because the left side of my body was weak, making the chair difficult to control. People did stare or snicker when I couldn't talk clearly making being social even more difficult. Rarely did anyone offer to help!

Trying to reconnect with old friends not only proved more difficult but also very disappointing. My friends saw me as somebody "different" from the person they had previously known. I wasn't the energetic constantly on-the-go person who could work all day and party all night that they remembered. Many of my longtime friends couldn't manage the adjustment. I was "changed." Friends that I had known for years and even some of my former military co-workers all came up with the same reaction and slowly began drifting away. I was on my own!

Since the bus stop was right on the corner in front of my new home, I started exploring the neighborhood. Within a short time I found there was a small non-profit agency nearby, Phoenix Shanti, which was accepting volunteers to help in their office. The agency ran a homeless & rehabilitation shelter along with varied health service programs for the indigent. They did accept volunteers if you met their rigid qualifications and went through a training program.

Remembering what the physical therapist had told me at Fort Hood, that if I wanted to get better mentally & physically I needed to find someone worse off than I was and help him. I needed to keep busy mentally and physically in order for my body to heal. After a rigorous set of interviews from the Shanti staff and a four-day orientation I entered their training program. At first I only worked a couple of hours a week as a volunteer file clerk. It was a refreshing change! Within a couple of weeks, the Senior Social Worker, Deloris, asked if I could increase my hours in the office. I was exhausted every day and constantly fighting pain yet for some reason I felt safer there than if I had just stayed home.

After a couple of months I was spending several days a week helping them out and I realized that many of my old talents were slowly returning. My speech and physical strength had improved also. I felt good about my life again! Meanwhile, two roommates at the house helped on chores and the expenses. My body was slowly improving physically though I still had the permanent 24-hour migraine which was 'controlled' by heavy medications and the TENS. The severe leg pains with muscle spasms at the end of the day were a different story. Not much I could do about them except to just keep on going and accepting the pain as part of my daily routine. The medications helped though their side effects could cause more problems.

Roommates came and went as I became more active in my daily life. The Veteran's Administration finally approved the disability claim for military injuries after I asked for assistance from the Disabled Veterans of America Service Officer. I received my first payment as 100% service connected disability from the VA almost two years to the day after I was retired from active duty. Social Security Disability had been awarded to me six months after I left the Fort Hood hospital and the Army had been giving me only 50% retirement pay when I left Fort Hood. Now I would receive full retirement pay and complete medical care. I could even afford to pay all of my bills without counting pennies at the end of the month and could now start paying off some of the credit cards that had been maxed-out while waiting on the disability claim.

Finally I was able to spend all day doing things without falling asleep or having to take a late afternoon nap. My clarity of speech had returned to normal, as long as I did not allow myself to become overly stressed. Using a cane or the walker was easier though stairs were almost impossible to climb. As part of the volunteer work at Phoenix Shanti, I had become involved in the local health care agencies and their continuing battle with the city & state over funding of services. To my surprise, the Shanti CEO Randy Gorbett, asked me to participate in a series of local meetings on health care & the homeless as his representative and to meet with a couple of the Arizona State legislators to discuss upcoming legislation and the needs of his organization.

Barely a month later Roxanne Snyder, Shanti's Housing Director, asked if I was interested in becoming a resident manager for one of their homeless shelters. They would provide an apartment with the utilities paid; all I had to do was keep track of the residents. Since my lease was up for renewal on the house it seemed like a perfect opportunity to save money, pay bills and Shanti would even provide me lunch & dinner at the shelter. The job lasted a year as my strength, coordination, and speech continued to improve. Phoenix Shanti also provided additional free counseling that had not been available at the Veteran's Hospital as compensation for the volunteer work which helped considerably. Their help and constant support kept me going and made a tremendous difference in my recovery. I shall always be grateful to their staff.

Approaching the three-year mark of forced retirement from the army, there were more changes. I had discovered that my father was using my disability trust fund as collateral for some of his business ventures. After a quick visit to an attorney, Social Security and the VA were convinced that I was competent to manage my own affairs. Father was very upset when Social Security & the VA took the money out of his control! A local bank provided assistance in setting up a Personal Trust Fund, checking & savings accounts and an investment portfolio.

I attended a conference on homeless issues in Washington D.C., representing Shanti and several local Arizona agencies in April 1993. As part of the conference, we visited with a few of the legislators, talking about the issues important to us. Washington D.C. and the surrounding area had a great subway & bus system! My strength had returned enough that I could use a cane or rolling walker for short distances as long as I took short breaks. This small amount of progress had made a tremendous difference in my ability to interact with people on an equal basis. Utilizing the training from the military, my skills in public speaking and a passion for advocacy, I was successful in accomplishing our goals for this conference. Returning to Phoenix I was highly energized and able to report good results.

About six months later Randy Gorbett took me to lunch one day, over desert he made a proposal that would be difficult to turn down. Randy asked if I would be interested in going back to Washington D.C. and representing Phoenix Shanti and a consortium of local health care agencies on a full time basis. I could not receive pay from Shanti or the consortium because of my disability pension but they would gladly pay for an apartment in exchange for the volunteer work. Randy had some friends in Washington that would assist me with introductions if I was interested in taking the position. I moved to Washington, D.C. almost one year to the day from when I attended that first conference in 1993.

Spending four years in Washington D.C., living in an apartment overlooking Arlington National Cemetery and the Pentagon on the Virginia side of the Potomac River taught me a lot about our political system. Don't ever let anyone kid you; politics is a very rough & dirty business! A nearby Veteran's Administration Hospital in the District was readily available via the subway and bus system. The VA primary care doctor from the D.C. hospital immediately enrolled me in several counseling & physical therapy programs when he realized the Phoenix VA Hospital had failed to do so when I was first retired. I did not tell him that Phoenix Shanti had provided some very valuable counseling and physical therapy while I was volunteering with them!

Whenever possible, I would spend part of each day at the many different museums looking at the exhibits. Washington was a beautiful city as long as you stayed within the tourist corridor, but absolute slums away from the tourist areas. The greatest drawback for me was the high humidity in the summer and six months of cold in the winter. The difference in the weather took a bit of adjustment since I was used to a much warmer and drier climate. Arriving with light-weight winter clothing, I had to scramble to find inexpensive but warm winter clothes. Fort Meyer Army Base, which provided support personnel for Arlington National Cemetery and other facilities in the area, had a great thrift shop where I did most of my shopping. The back gate for Fort Meyer was only one block from my apartment so access was easy. Using the Exchange & Commissary at Fort Meyer also saved a lot of money on household goods and groceries.

Those four years were very special. The assistance from the VA hospital made a big difference, especially with improvements in the various pain medications and the counseling. My body was regaining strength, memory was improving, and I felt alive inside. Some occasions and activities in Washington I do remember with fondness. I spent a lot of time attending Congressional seminars & luncheons, talking with influential leaders of our country and eventually receiving recognition for doing something important on a few projects. In the end I had a large binder full of letters and photographs from various members of Congress and people that I had worked with. Even President Clinton wrote me a few letters!

Participating in various conferences and activities were a requirement of the job as lobbyist/advocate and I became involved in as many of them as possible. Surprisingly, the physical activity was helping me to slowly gain strength as my body was continuing to heal itself. I still suffered with the constant migraine, pain in my legs and sometimes slurred speech. However, I had learned to allow myself "down days" to revitalize and recharge.

I was honored to participate in several Veterans Day parades in both Washington D.C. and New York City. The two greatest occasions were being in the 50th Anniversary Veteran's Day Parade in New York City when the Assistant to the Mayor of Manhattan Borough pushed my wheelchair in the parade through ice & snow. When the parade paused in front of Saint Patrick's Cathedral, Cardinal John O'Conner came down the church steps and shook my hand. Cardinal O'Conner then posed for a photo, standing beside me. That photo even made one of the New York City newspapers! At the end of the parade it took four men to pry me out of the wheelchair and place me in a taxi. The wool Dress Blue army uniform had literally frozen itself to the wheelchair. That uniform was great for cold weather and because of all the gold braid it looked fantastic for parades. However, when it became wet the uniform did not dry easily, acting like a sponge. I spent two weeks recuperating from that parade and it was worth every minute!

Then on Memorial Day 1995 as part of a six-person group of veterans, we joined over one hundred other groups that day presenting wreaths at the Tomb of The Unknown Soldiers in Washington D.C. The laying of the wreaths had started at 8a.m. with President Clinton making the symbolic visit and wreath presentation early that morning. We had to wait until 3p.m. to make our presentation but it was such an honor! I had spent all day in my wheelchair and knew that I could not use my cane or walker during the presentation so my friend SSG Miriam BenShalom held my arm to help me navigate the steps.

I would like to think that I did some good work while in Washington though I realized after a while that politics was a cut-throat business. During the Clinton Administration, as a Contributor to the President's Commission to Investigate the Gulf War Illness, I saw several examples of 'dirty politics' that really upset me. Since the Veteran's Administration had not declared Gulf War Illness to be legit, those suffering from unknown problems were ridiculed or badly treated. Quite often they were refused treatment! The results of the Commission weren't released until a couple of years later, which resulted in many veterans suffering needlessly. The Veteran's

Administration had acted the same way regarding Vietnam Vets & Agent Orange! Eventually, I found myself disillusioned and frustrated by the convoluted political process. Sadly realizing that if I continued the lobbying and advocacy work, compromising personal ethics and values would be inevitable! I knew it was time once more to make some changes in my life!

Sometime during the month of May 1997 I realized that I was losing my effectiveness at the job and that it was no longer fun. It was time to leave Washington! I found that preparing to return to Arizona would actually be quite easy. The process seemed very quick and simple once I made up my mind to leave the political arena and return to Arizona. Friends had the look of disbelief when they heard I was giving up my apartment, buying an old motor home, and going back to Arizona. A friend had volunteered to drive me if I would pay for his return plane ticket back to Virginia. He was also going to teach me how to drive again, in case there was an emergency. Giving away some of my excess furniture was actually fun! Saying good-by to some of my friends was not so easy.

We took two months of commuting between Virginia and my hometown in North Carolina to fix most of the problems with that old motor home and in the process I had tried to reconnect with my mother. Since Father died from the brain tumor in 1995 she had remained in Plymouth. Her family members had become very frustrated trying to care for her. Mother was showing signs of dementia along with her schizophrenia that was usually out of control. Attempting to negotiate a better living situation for her after his death wasn't easy. When the day came for her to move across the street to a newly remodeled home, she refused and demanded that I leave her house. She accused me of trying to steal her "valuable furniture," when in truth I was trying to loan her some of my furniture that I had from my apartment in Virginia. My friend and I hurriedly packed up the motor home and headed for Arizona!

Quickly discovering the fifteen-year-old 27-foot motor home had never been intended or designed for full time living. Preparing for the long trip west as I tried to cram all of my possessions inside

143

became a nightmare. There was no room left for modification! It was overloaded inside, leaving just enough room for one person to sit at the dining table and I had to crawl over boxes to get into bed at night. My friend insisted that the partially reclining driver's seat was a comfortable bed though every morning he had a sore back. It must have been quite a sight as the overloaded motor home pulling a sixteen-foot trailer full of furniture and boxes and making all sorts of noise as it rolled down the highway.

The old engine only got about five miles to the gallon of gas. All sorts of things kept breaking or intermittently working. Old plastic water lines kept breaking every couple of days so I was constantly dealing with wet carpet. By the time we got to Phoenix, we had installed a new transmission, six new tires, two water pumps, multiple water leaks repaired inside, a new refrigerator, the generator was rebuilt, repaired holes in the roof twice, a new toilet & dump tanks, and a new windshield. I had been fortunate in putting out two small electrical fires before there was serious damage! Still the engine was failing as we rolled into Phoenix on a hot afternoon on the tenth of August.

At first the little motor home was parked in the side yard of an old army friend, Chuck Boggs, for a couple of months in Phoenix. Sadly, I found that it hadn't been a very wise choice as Chuck and his wife Nina, were going through a nasty divorce. The summer heat in Phoenix, which I had loved years before, seemed to suck the life and energy from me when I went outside. It was time to make a change! Packing up the motor home once more, placing some items into storage, I found that it would only run in first & second gears as we left Phoenix.

It was a very slow 70 mile journey up Interstate 17, driving most of the time in the emergency lane, we expected a ticket at any moment. After a frustrating hour of phone calls during lunch at the Golden Corral, I found a run-down but cheap trailer park outside Prescott that would accept my old motor home for a long term rental. I spent the next year in that park, unable to move the RV, putting up with the drunks and druggies next door while paying off bills and building up my credit. I had purchased an electric scooter in D.C. which became my only way to get around. Fortunately Prescott did have several taxi companies since there was no bus service for the area.

I continued to improve physically, walking in the foothills and exploring the Indian ruins that lay around Willow Lake. A new physical therapist was starting to work at the Prescott VA hospital. Debbie Molter immediately enrolled me in a rigorous program of physical therapy in her clinic. Her efforts contributed greatly to my rapid improvement over the next year. Crowded as it was, that motor home provided a roof over my head. I usually ignored the drunken neighbors and tried to avoid getting embroiled in personalities and petty politics within the trailer park. Unlike some of the residents, I knew that I would eventually leave that park and live in a better situation.

York RV was the largest RV dealership in the region and they were located half a mile down the street. I spent many afternoons looking at trailers, motor homes and talking with the sales manager Bob Been. Living in that old 27 footer had taught me a few lessons and I realized that I would either have to move into an apartment or into a much larger motor home. At that time there were very few apartments in Prescott and I certainly didn't want to return to Phoenix.

One day I saw this monster Winnebago Adventurer motor home on the back lot. It looked brand new, did not have any price stickers on it and when I looked inside it had everything that I could possibly want for full time living, including lots of storage space. Turns out it belonged to the sales manager Bob Been. He had bought it four months earlier, used it twice, and then had a fancy one awarded to him by Winnebago. Bob was planning to sell the customized coach at a discount. After several weeks of negotiating, I bought the motor home from Bob on 29 December 1998. As soon as word got out about the purchase, several friends were offering to drive just so they could travel or go camping.

Living full time in a quality travel coach is not only fun but also an adventure! We saw beautiful sights, great sunsets, sunrises, and discovered out of the way little places to park or camp that provided breath-taking views. One time I spent thirty days perched on the side of a cliff near the North Rim of the Grand Canyon. It was awesome! Another trip at 9,000 feet altitude nestled in the pine trees near the Colorado state line with elk grazing at the front door every evening. I rarely stayed in RV parks or resorts, usually choosing instead to 'boondock' and rough it so that I could enjoy the peaceful side of nature. Since the coach had a wonderful generator & battery system I never worried about power or taking care of my needs. It even had a built in telephone, satellite TV, and a music system. All of it was accessible inside or even out on the patio area.

A John Deere Gator ATV, which was pulled behind the motor home on a small trailer, provided my extra pair of legs and served as alternate transportation. The Gator was my way to explore and I even used it to go into town for groceries. It's amazing how many hidden canyons and beautiful sights are there for exploring when you get away from the main roads. Fortunately, the Gator had a fully enclosed steel cab with comfortable seats and glass windows so it was usable in all types of weather situations. It was easy on the gas too! Over the next couple of years the Gator made it through numerous snow & rain storms and navigated almost impassable ravines as I reconnoitered the back country with my medical service dog Buzz perched on the seat beside me. When I would get out of the Gator, Buzz jumped into my driver's seat, looking like he was ready to drive when I returned.

That wonderful Winnebago coach provided a great home until I had my first heart attack in a little place called Quartzsite, Arizona during the winter of 2004. We had been getting ready for a return trip to Alaska when it happened. Fortunately there was a VA extension clinic up the road at Lake Havasu City. The primary care physician, Doctor Arevalo, after an extensive exam, said that I shouldn't travel for a few months, so I spent the next twelve months in Quartzsite instead of going to Alaska. Then two more mild heart attacks within a six month period had Doctor Arevalo worried because other symptoms were showing up which she couldn't explain. She pressured me to move closer to a regular hospital so after several house hunting trips I found a place in Lake Havasu City and put the motor home up for sale.

Several months later, in October 2006, I woke up one morning and found I couldn't get out of bed. I was very weak; my legs were numb, and unable to walk. Using the walker to stand up was difficult if not impossible at times. After considerable effort I crawled to the bathroom and spent the remainder of the day in the recliner in the living room. Fortunately I was able to park my electric scooter next to the recliner and use it to get around inside the house. After a frantic sct of phone calls to Doctor Arevalo and several trips over the next few months to see specialists, the increasing medical problems still perplexed the doctors. Thanks to Doctor Arevalo, a Social Worker quickly arranged for the delivery of meals, housekeeping service, and a visiting nurse checked on me every week.

I kept hoping that my condition would improve and I could return to a more normal life but that didn't happen. We continued testing for two more months and finally one day Doctor Arevalo thought she had enough solid data. She forwarded all of the test results to the regional VA hospital in Prescott. Their devastating decisions changed my life forever! The Prescott VA Hospital told Doctor Arevalo that they wanted me to move into a nursing home located in Sedona within the next two weeks!

They were convinced that I had a progressive and terminal form of Parkinson's disease which would cause incapacitation and death very quickly. The Prescott doctors believed my present medical condition would rapidly worsen so I had to be placed into a facility as soon as possible. Since I was "terminal" the Veteran's Administration would cover the complete cost of my care. However, the move meant that I had to give up all of my worldly possessions and be prepared to die within six months to a year, suffering further physical and mental decline. My life seemed destined to come to an abrupt end once again!

No one had wanted to buy the motor home so I called the bank, asking for assistance and advice. After a lengthy discussion it was decided that I should allow the bank to make an immediate voluntary repossession. Once it was sold at auction, I would pay off the difference. That killed my credit rating! It took three days to unload and dispose of all the camping and travel gear inside the motor home before it was picked up.

Luckily, there was a UPS Store nearby which provided some wonderful help. I donated several boxes of military memorabilia to two different museums, all of the letters and documents from my work in Washington were given to another. There were two foot lockers full of commercial airline documents and paraphernalia that dated back to the 1940s, a home for them was found at the Clark

County-Cannon Aviation Museum near Las Vegas. Mementoes I'd collected from trips overseas were donated to several individuals and my antique German Beer Stein collection decorated a shelf in one of the finer Lake Havasu City restaurants. Several of my Army uniforms were donated to the Prescott VA Hospital for display. To have achieved so much in my life and then to have it end abruptly just didn't seem fair! Still the mystic fates had other plans for my future.

CHAPTER FIFTEEN

SEDONA, ARIZONA
JOAN/SISTER JOSE—AUGUST 2008

The search for more information on Jimmie Hobday continued and the phone conversations with Joan/Sister Jose became longer and more involved. Unfortunately her worsening medical condition made it difficult at times. Her sudden decision to stop or delay plans to honor Jimmie caused problems on many levels. While talking with the Air Force Funeral Division, located in San Antonio, Texas, I was fortunate to find a woman who was Catholic, Marian Fischer, who explained some of the "finer points" of her Faith as she has an older sister that was also a Nun.

When Marian contacted Jimmie's sister Joan/Sister Jose again, it took two hours of delicate phone conversation, for them to reach an agreement. Sister Jose would agree to let the Air Force proceed in honoring her brother Jimmie if they put his gravestone at Arlington National Cemetery instead of his hometown of Cortez. She also decided to sell the three remaining cemetery plots in Cortez and possibly having her mothers' gravestone upgraded by adding Jimmie and his older brother Richard's names to the stone.

This threw a brick into all of the plans for a large military funeral made by her fellow classmates, and other folks in the town of Cortez. Then in a telephone conversation with Sister Jose, she asked me "Who are the 40s Bunch"? I replied "Sister, they are your high school classmates that were your friends and Jimmie's too. They feel very strongly about honoring him and you after all these years." Her comment shocked me! "I remember attending their 50th Graduation Anniversary. Those people don't really care about Jimmie or me! They don't really know either one of us!" With that, Sister Jose said I had been a good friend, thanked me for the assistance and that this was "Good-By" and hung up the phone. So much for trying to tell her that I was Jimmie's son!

I called Marian at the Air Force Funeral Division and relayed the conversation. She said I should not worry. A directive from her headquarters had already listed me as Jimmie's son. In the future the Air Force Casualty Office & the Funeral Services Office would send me copies of everything sent to his sister. The Air Force had made the decision based on all of the documentation that I had sent them, plus our telephone conversations. If Sister Jose failed to show up at the Arlington National Cemetery Memorial Ceremony, scheduled for next April, then they would take alternative actions. Her recognition and acceptance of me as Jimmie's son was not a requirement though it would make their job easier.

After much deliberation I decided to take a dangerous course of action on 11 September 2008. I wrote a letter to Bishop Kicanas, he was in charge of the Catholic Diocese in Tucson. Since this was where Sister Jose served I was hoping for assistance, but not really expecting to receive any reply. Without mentioning her name I loosely described my situation. A Nun under his supervision was possibly my Aunt and that due to her illness I was hesitant in discussing the matter on the telephone with her. As I saw it, this was my last chance to meet with Sister Jose and discuss the situation! Her acknowledgment most of all would be of great value emotionally to me.

"Your Grace, I have known the Nun in question, for several months and talked with her by phone, and corresponded with her. She only knows me as someone that once lived in the town where she went to school and that I was doing some research on the internet when I found that she had been a neighbor and was still alive . . .

My intentions have been honorable, and not to deceive, but such a matter as this is not the type of thing you just say on the telephone or write in a letter . . . When I learned how seriously ill she was it just reinforced the fact that I not only had to wait until she was in better health, but also not to alarm her or unduly upset her.

I have been involved in correcting government records for one of her family members. Unfortunately, inquiry postings I had placed in various web sites were recently discovered by people that know the Sister. They have recently contacted me and after long discussion, accepted the fact that I wanted to be able to tell the Sister personally, rather than someone else, about the family connection. Her friends have promised not to tell the Sister; though there is always the chance someone else will find the same postings and notify the Sister of the listing.

Once I start describing in detail, you would instantly know exactly which Nun I am writing about which is why I am being a bit vague at this time. I do not wish to cause undue alarm or pain to her and as a result, am very apprehensive about providing specific information until I know I may work confidentially through you or your designate.

What I desire most is that over time, directly or through your appointee, her health, & mental status can be monitored so that one day the Sister can be told that many years ago her younger brother had a son born out of wedlock. Now that child is a grown man who would like to meet and talk with her . . . When the Sister took her vows she "put away the past & locked it in a closet" and she will have to unlock the closet in order to deal with this situation . . . If she is not agreeable or in good enough health, I will drop this matter and consider it closed. At this time I have no family to claim me, no hometown to claim and am living near her in another part of Arizona." The last sentence in the letter read, "I do not and will not do anything to cause her mental distress or create a problem medically for her."

Over the next couple of months, Sister Jose frequently changed her mind on several things. Including what she wanted done at the hometown cemetery in Cortez. At the last moment she did call the Air Force Casualty Office, confirming her plans to attend the Family Update Conference presented by the Pentagon in October. The Air Force even offered to take her to on a tour of Arlington National Cemetery and show her where the gravestone would be placed for Jimmie. Unknown to the Air Force or me, her medical condition was deteriorating rapidly.

Since I had previously lived a few blocks from the Pentagon and right next to Arlington National Cemetery, I knew that the pomp & ceremony would be considerably more than what had been planned in Jimmie's hometown of Cortez. Joan had felt those plans were "too much" saying that all she wanted was a very simple ceremony. I seriously thought that if Sister Jose makes it to the Washington Conference, once she sees the pomp & ceremony at Arlington Cemetery, she wouldn't return later. God willing, I'm going to be there somehow for the actual Memorial Ceremony! Whether it's standing quietly in the background or sitting in the front row with Sister Jose as she is receiving the Burial Flag and Presentation Case.

Sister Jose and I continued to develop our friendship during our phone calls and shared many personal feelings but I never had the courage or felt secure enough to tell her about our possible relationship. It was just too personal a thing to talk about over the phone! Rationalizing my actions by concluding that if Joan, Sister Jose, never allows me to tell her the truth, then it will be her loss in the end! Dying, as the "last of the family line" noble and stubborn.

Without ever knowing that her brother whom she had loved so dearly had brought a son into this world, a nephew that she could have been proud of, and I would have given her my unconditional love in return. I don't pretend to understand her Catholic faith, though I respect her beliefs and feelings. However, the rules, attitudes, and rituals of the Catholic Church confused me at times.

I went back over the messages stored in my telephone and found that I had luckily saved her "good-by" call. As I listened to the conversation again, I heard a sentence that I had ignored before, in her deep oratorical voice "I have consulted with my doctor and with my Priest. Both of them have advised me to divest myself of all these memories and pains as they are the reasons I am having health problems." The answer had been there all along!

That letter I sent to Bishop Kicanas, asking for his assistance but not naming the Nun involved. He didn't answer by mail! Instead, two weeks after sending the letter, Bishop Kicanas called on my private phone line and asked for me by name! I had not given my complete name or my phone number in the vague message that I had sent him! Just enough information to get his attention, so he must be her Priest! She had Confessed, her fears, the past, and the truth to him. Only Sister Jose could have given the Bishop my unlisted phone number. Bishop Kicanas had politely said in his phone call that it was up to the Nun to make the first move or to become involved in family matters. Bishop Kicanas said that he didn't want to become personally involved in the matter "unless it caused her health problems or if the Nun specifically requested his involvement."

Sister Jose must realize who I am! Her training as a Nun and devotion to her Church was possibly so deep that it was preventing her from accepting, or even recognizing my existence! Her lack of action made it appear as though Sister Jose was hiding behind the cloak of the Convent & the Church rather than accepting or dealing with the truth! With any luck this would be proven wrong. Unless something unexpected happens, Sister Jose would go to her grave with the secret, without accepting or acknowledging my existence.

Is that why she said, "All of this brings up too many old ghosts"? We had come so far yet a chasm that I could not breach seemed to stretch before us!

Today is October 16; Sister Mary Jose (Joan) Hobday should have gone to the Washington D.C. Survivors Conference. Will I get a report from the Air Force on how things went? Did she change her mind on what the Air Force would do for Jimmie in the future? Did the Air Force or Casualty Office representatives tell her anything about me?

The Air Force Casualty Branch at the Pentagon called early the next morning. Sister Jose did go! She enjoyed the conference! Sister Jose also approved of the program proposed for Arlington National Cemetery by the Casualty Office. It was still difficult to think of her as a Nun, in my mind she would always be Joan. Upon her arrival in Washington D.C., the Casualty Office had given Sister Jose the royal treatment. They had even taken her to visit the Basilica at Catholic University for her prayer time. Apparently the visit to the Viet Nam Wall and a private tour of Arlington National Cemetery made the difference. Sister Jose felt that honoring Jimmie in this way was the right thing to do. It took very little convincing after Sister Jose stood on the hillside where Jimmie's memorial stone was to be placed. His headstone would be alongside other Korean War veterans and she could see that the Air Force and Cemetery representatives were very serious about honoring Jimmie in a proper manner.

There is always the chance Sister Jose may not be able to make it back for the Memorial Ceremony at Arlington National Cemetery due to her declining health. The Air Force Casualty Office reassured me that as Jimmie's son I was entitled to participate and to represent "the family" at the Memorial Ceremony if Joan doesn't show up. If she does go, and we have not been able to tell her who I am, I will probably just stand quietly in the background. However, in conversation it seemed that the Air Force really wanted me to be present and participate in the Memorial Ceremony!

Of all the thoughts rolling around inside my head, the one that hurt the most was that I have gone through this life journey alone and that I may never see it completed. For some reason beyond my comprehension I felt that I had to finish this task! However, for the first time in my life, something unexpected has been added to the equation. I felt a strong connection with the people in Cortez, the high school classmates of Jimmie & Joan Hobday. On the phone and in their letters, those folks make me feel like they have adopted me as one of their own and that I am wanted! I've been accepted as Jimmie Hobday's son and welcomed into their hearts. Just the thought gives me chills after a lifetime of holding this secret shame inside and knowing that there was no one out there that cared about me as a person, as a member of a family much less a town.

Possibly, by the time I die Cortez will be my "hometown" and I'll be able to rest knowing that those folks will not forget me. Becky, the Cortez Cemetery director, says there is a plot reserved for me in their Veterans Section if I want it. The Veteran's Administration would provide a headstone upon my death and ship it to Cortez. An idea began to roll around in my head. After some research I found it would be easy to make plans for a bronze plaque to be placed in the ground or on my gravestone, honoring my dad (Jimmie), and his fellow B-29 crewmembers. Becky says that will be okay and not go against Joan's wishes and still be within the Veteran's Administration guidelines for burial.

A few days later as I was returning from lunch in the nursing home dining room, a package arrived in the mail from Sister Jose. She had sent two more of her books, one on living a simple stress free life and the other a collection of short stories about her childhood. Spending the next few days reading her books, thinking about this whole situation and the upcoming Memorial Ceremony in Cortez for John Spruell, provided a fresh outlook and possibly a different approach to handling some of the issues that plagued me. Calmed by Sister Jose's words and reenergized, I started to write down my thoughts about the revelations on Jimmie and my life. It helped put everything into perspective. The discovery of that envelope with the pictures and letters inside had changed my life forever!

156

CHAPTER SIXTEEN

-DANE-December 2008-

The gravestone for John Spruell arrived in Cortez three weeks before the Memorial Ceremony. The Spruell family decided that the Ceremony should be held on 6 Dec 2008, which was 58 years to the day after his death. A fitting tribute and since it was on a Saturday, that should also make it easier for folks to attend. The Spruell family had no idea of where to start with some of the preparations so they asked me to assist on the organization of things. The local American Legion Post & the Veterans of Foreign Wars Post were also helping them coordinate activities. This would be a challenging task for everyone. Especially for me, since I was several hundred miles away from Cortez and living in a nursing home. With everyone working together and combining their talents we might just get things organized and the ceremony would be successful.

My greatest contribution would be my knowledge of how to work with government agencies and access to the internet. I began to send notices out via email and letters to all of the military & veteran's organizations. Even including the nearby Colorado military bases in the mail outs, hoping they might want to become involved. Then one of the webmasters for a popular veteran's site picked it up. He sent an email stating that he had put the Memorial Ceremony announcement on the "active military circuit" so every military command and base around the world would know about it. Even the military newspapers were receiving a copy of the notice. Nothing was being left to chance! Contacting all of the veteran's organizations that I had built up a level of communication with, hoping that somehow, someway, a few folks would respond. Any type of participation or recognition would validate John Spruell's sacrifice either by them sending flowers, Letters of Condolence or by some miracle showing up at the Cortez Memorial Service.

Both the Spruell family and I started receiving inquiries and final answers from several organizations & individuals. There were two big issues creating a problem. Cortez was in the mountains, it was winter with potential snow & blizzard conditions, and it was over a hundred miles from the nearest 'big city'. Many of the folks offered their condolences but really didn't want to travel the distance, especially in the winter. It was a difficult feeling to explain, but in my heart I wanted the Spruell family to have what Joan/Sister Jose had denied herself and Jimmie. I wanted them to be able to remember and to be proud of their distant relative, Corporal John Spruell. For them to pass on to future generations that someone in the Spruell family had sacrificed his life in a faraway place just because his Country asked him to go there. A true war hero! Most of the Spruell family wasn't even born when CPL John Spruell went to Korea!

After weeks of trying, contact was finally made with some of the Marine Detachments that had been at Hagaru-ri or other parts of the Chosin Reservoir in Korea. I even found a couple of 7th Infantry websites. However, I learned very fast, some of those websites were started years earlier and just left running on the internet with no one really monitoring them on a full time basis. This resulted in minimal exposure or participation, so that the posted inquiries may only be read by a few people.

Then I was blindsided by the local newspaper in Cortez, the publisher, Suzy Meyer who had been my long distance confidant & 'friend' for nine months, suddenly said: "People that have been dead for 58 years are not news, no one around here will want to hear about it, or care about it." We ended up in a bit of a tiff as a result. Suzy didn't want to print anything on the upcoming events, even going so far as to omitting the announcement from the Veteran's Day coverage in the newspaper. Dennis Spruell and his family were stymied too as it seemed that she was suddenly "too busy to talk to him." or anyone else in their family.

I asked Dennis for permission to see if I could pull a couple of strings as long as the resulting actions didn't hurt him, his family or cause problems for the Memorial Ceremony and he agreed to let me try. The next day a long email letter was sent to three national veteran's organizations, and one to the owner in Denver of the Cortez newspaper, advising him of my actions & why. As much as I would like to claim full responsibility and credit, the ensuing bombardment of phone calls, emails and letters from people all over the United States made the difference. Their actions actually helped to resolve the situation. The Spruell family was also working diligently to make arrangements and getting things organized in Cortez.

One reply that was forwarded to the Cortez newspaper as well as their owner in Denver was an email sent to me by Major General Mason C. Whitney who was the Director of the Colorado Governor's Office of Homeland Security on 13 November 2008.

"Dane . . . It is up to all of us veterans to ensure our communities remember those of us who didn't return after they answered their nation's call. It is even more important today since most Americans don't realize the sacrifices that are made by our great men and women in uniform because our military is so small today compared to the military you and I grew up in and most American's aren't connected to the military as a result. Keep up the good work of jogging the memories of those who are supposed to tell our veterans' stories so their sacrifices won't be forgotten. Regards, MG (Retired) Mason C. Whitney"

Later I learned that the next day Suzy had greeted Dennis Spruell with all smiles and full cooperation! I began the work I had really wanted to do, contacting the remaining survivors of the Chosin Few veteran's organization and trying to get some type of participation from them. The Chosin Few Association had recently closed down their National Headquarters. The Association was now operating out of a smaller location as too many of the old soldiers were dying off or were too sick to be involved on a full time basis. Thousands of men died around the Chosin Reservoir and now only a few hundred of the survivors were still alive. Corporal John Spruell was part of that legacy and should be honored as such!

Dennis Spruell mentioned in an email that the cemetery was going to be setting the marble gravestone marker that the VA had sent them for John Spruell into the ground sometime in the next week. Suddenly I had an inspiration! The family needed something they could really identify with. Something that would be symbolic of their uncle John! The next morning I mailed them a small package with a letter attached.

"Dennis, I felt that something was missing. Possibly a symbolic memento placed into the gravesite when they set the stone, something that would be symbolic of John's service and sacrifice. Something that would remain forever as part of his legacy since his body will not be present. If you agree and are comfortable with it, I have enclosed a small case holding a few tokens.

Each item represents a part of the military, the Army, and our remembrance of John. Attached is a Combat Infantryman's Badge, John earned that along with all of the other military men that died or served in the Korean War. Normally this award is issued to those who serve in combat. However, Congress declared that because it was a "United Nations Police Action," those men who served or died in that conflict are not entitled to the award! Most of the active duty & retired military men and women in this nation, past and present, strongly disagree! This is a symbol of what he earned and surely deserved. An Army signet ring is also enclosed. It is a symbol of his service to this country. Something he earned but never had the chance to wear. The two military coins represent the Honor & Service to his country and to God. The ribbon that is around the small case represents our promise to John Spruell that we will never forget him or his ultimate sacrifice."

Eventually, just over two weeks before the Memorial Ceremony I had another break, Pete Hildre a member of the Denver Chapter of the Chosin Few, saw the posting I made to one of the websites, asking for assistance in contacting chapter members. Pete called early one morning and offered to send me an old copy of his chapter's membership roster. He didn't know if very many of the men were still alive or their current health, but it was worth a try. Pete did have the name of the man that had taken over the National Headquarters operations for the Chosin Few Association, Don Gee.

Don was still trying to keep a line of communication open amongst the Chosin Few members. A phone call with several follow-up emails to Don Gee provided additional support and advice. I typed out a form letter, plugged in names from the Chosin Few membership roster and sent out personal invitations to each person, requesting that if they couldn't attend to consider sending flowers for the Ceremony or a Letter of Condolence to the family. Everything possible had been done. We were going to have to wait and see who responded and who showed up.

I began to think about what I could say at the Memorial Ceremony in a limited amount of time that would mean the most, for the family and for those persons in attendance. I felt very strongly that this Memorial Ceremony should give Corporal John Spruell the honor he deserved in his hometown of Cortez. The current members of the Spruell family needed this ceremony to bring balance and closure to this part of their family history. His family could be proud of him and the events would be something tangible that they could pass on to their grandchildren. Finally John Spruell would have recognition as a true Korean War Hero. It would also provide the Cortez area with a signature event that might help other local veterans and their families in the future. I was sure there had to be other forgotten soldiers from the Cortez area that should be honored also. After all, there was an old saying that I firmly believed in: "Soldiers take care of Soldiers."

-3 December 2008-

Things have been very hectic, sad at times and even surprising. Suzy Meyer and her Cortez newspaper started blaming me, stating that I was not a local resident therefore I did not and should not have anything to do with the Spruell's Memorial Ceremony. Several of the local & national veteran's groups banded together and started putting pressure on the newspaper. Suzy's actions were causing confusion and delays as well as making me feel frustrated and unwanted. Many defeatist thoughts ran through my head while I was sitting in that nursing home room. I was ready to throw in the towel and just cancel my plans, letting the folks in Cortez go it alone. Possibly the only solution was to remove myself totally from the situation. Perhaps I had been wrong to get involved. I had been alone all of my life, I guess I could continue that way!

Suddenly emails and letters started pouring in; maybe things were going to work out after all! Veteran's groups from around the United States began to send dozens of emails; people began to send letters, emails, and gifts to the Spruell family. The Cortez chapters of the American Legion & Veterans of Foreign Wars were doing everything they could to take care of local activities. The Denver television stations wanted to cover the event. An anonymous donor set up a Memorial Fund in John Spruell's name at the Cortez cemetery. The fund would help keep the Veteran's Section of the cemetery clean, repaired and even provide for assistance to those that could not afford a plot. Several chapters of The Chosin Few & AUSA Officers associations were sending large wreaths and putting out notices to their members. The State Adjutant for Governor Ritter of Colorado called, saying they were sending down an Honors Team for the Flag Presentation, a Rifle Team & a bugler. Was a motel available and could they handle a bus full of soldiers?

The Memorial Ceremony was coming together at the very last moment! I felt a giant weight lift off me and it was great! Now I had to get ready for the trip. The nursing home director was not comfortable with the idea of going on a trip but she said if my doctors had no objections then she would not stand in my way. Buzz & I could fly from Prescott to Cortez with only one change in airplanes. Service Dogs were allowed to fly free and he would be able to sit next to me in the plane. Rather than take the small electric travel scooter I decided just to take my folding walker to make it easier when changing planes in Farmington, New Mexico. Great Lakes commuter airline used a 12 seat aircraft that had very small seats and the plane ride was going to be rough and bumpy. It would probably feel like an old DC-3 but with less room and nowhere to stand.

Arriving early at the Prescott airport the morning of departure gave me time to talk with a couple of airport workers about the changes the airfield had seen since I lived there as a child. Though we were delayed in Farmington, New Mexico for an hour we arrived in Cortez only one-half hour late. Buzz handled the plane ride and noise as though he had been flying all of his life. The small twelve-seat plane landed at the Cortez Municipal airport late that winter afternoon and a wave of deja vu swept over me as I remembered tidbits from my childhood.

Here was the town where I was conceived. I was about to meet people that had known my real dad! It was about an hour before sunset as I walked into the air terminal. Sunlight, breaking through the grey clouds was catching the snow-capped peaks in the distance. The air was clean, cool, and crisp. I called Chuck Haley to let him know I'd arrived and then took Buzz for a walk outside. Buzz was happy to be on the ground and enjoyed snuffling around in the snow while we were waiting. He loved to play in the snow but this wasn't the time or place.

Chuck & Marilyn Haley arrived shortly. They wanted to take Buzz & I out to dinner rather than Marilyn cooking at home. They were eager to fill me in on all of the local gossip and activities concerning the upcoming Memorial Ceremony for John Spruell. As we drove through town Chuck was pointing out various landmarks, adding in tidbits on local events. Marilyn chipped in occasionally about people or activities. The conversation was going so well I didn't even notice that we had already arrived at the restaurant. We were seated at a long picnic-bench style table with a red & white checkered tablecloth. The small country style diner they had chosen quickly served up our orders. I was hungry and had no problem consuming the oversized chicken fried steak dinner.

Buzz was his usual self, quietly lying under the dining table during the entire meal. When we put our coats on to leave the waitress commented that she had not even noticed Buzz. She said I was fortunate to have such a well-behaved dog. I was very tired so when we arrived at their home, Chuck offered a bedtime hot chocolate and I quickly fell asleep in their guest room, with Buzz curled up on the floor beside the bed. Later that night he did sneak up on the bed and lay beside me for a while.

The next morning Chuck drove Buzz & I over to my old home, the McNeil house, just four blocks away. Chuck had been able to locate the house by the photos I had sent him, even to where I had been standing as a toddler when the photos were taken. We visited the vacant lots where Jimmie's home had been and the house where John Spruell had lived. He kept up a running commentary on some of the activities the boys had been involved in when they were in high school as we slowly drove down the small tree lined streets. Pointing out various landmarks and providing wonderful tidbits about some of the friends and classmates from their school days. I began to feel as though I'd been right there with them during their childhood.

After lunch we stopped to meet the Spruell family and go over the Memorial Ceremony plans and activities for the next day. The Spruell's, like Chuck & Marilyn, were friendly folks who immediately made me feel at home. Dennis Spruell was proud to show off a large print of the POW-MIA National Memorial near Pearl Harbor, which they had just received in the mail from the Hawaii Disabled Veterans of America Commander. A close up photo of the marble tiles with the names of John Spruell & Jimmie Hobday had been included along with a nice letter from the DAV Commander. I was amazed at the stack of letters and emails on the kitchen table that the family had received in the last few weeks! The entire family was excited about all of the recognition and attention that this "forgotten uncle" had created.

Dennis was very proud of a four page letter sent to him by Jim Westendorf who was a Chosin Survivor and member of the 1st Marine Division. His story was similar to so many of the letters, only it seemed to be more emotional and vivid. Jim had sent a copy of the letter to me and still to this day every time I read it my eyes tear up.

"I myself Dennis, am a survivor of the battle of the Chosin Reservoir . . . Dennis, even after all these long years, on certain occasions my thought will drift back to those epic few days in North Korea, now identified as the battle of the Chosin Reservoir, and what occurred there.

There is no way that I can adequately describe the horrors and destruction that both the weather and the Chi-coms (Chinese Communists) inflicted upon the brave & courageous Army and Marine Corps forces fighting for their lives, for their survival at that place. But 'we' and the weather wrought, extracted, a far greater measure of death & destruction upon them.

Dennis you have to know this.., the courage, the acts of valor and bravery, selfless courage, the determination to fight, to live, to survive to protect and help each other, just for another day . . . displayed by these troops was so very evident and uppermost in our minds and was the determining factor, despite seemingly impossible odds . . . we won out! But not without further suffering, wounds, freezing weather, frost-bite, hunger . . ., and unfortunately, the loss of more of us on the way out.

Obviously, and unfortunately, your Uncle John was one of many of those brave troopers and marines that fell in the battle of the

Chosin Reservoir . . . I think also, from what I knew at the time, and have subsequently learned the more of it, John was possibly one of the survivors of that horror, making his way back to Hagaru-ri with others of his outfit, many carrying, dragging, helping their wounded brethren, suffering further from frost-bite, from the terrible freezing weather, the biting wind, across the barren ice of the reservoir, in the pitch black of night . . . to finally make it back, safely, to the marine lines at Hagaru-ri. One can only imagine their plight, only to lose his life a few days later!

The manner in which your Uncle John fell is not known, but you can believe, he didn't 'give it up' cheaply. I think that you can take heart Dennis, in believing that John acted courageously, helping his mates, encouraging them along the way before he fell. You and your family can be very proud of your Uncle John . . . Jim Westendorf" . . . Such was the content of many of the emails and letters the Spruell family received.

Later that day Chuck & Dennis helped arrange for Buzz to see a local veterinarian while we were at the Memorial Ceremony. We would drop Buzz off as we left the house that morning so he could be examined during the Ceremony. While we were in the airplane I had discovered a lump on his right hip and was very concerned as he had been such a special companion to me. That dog had saved my life twice over the last ten years. Buzz always knew when I needed my medications or was about to have a seizure before I did. I owed him a lot and loved him dearly!

-SATURDAY 6 DECEMBER 2008—CORTEZ, COLORADO-

The day of the Spruell Memorial Ceremony had arrived. It was clear and cold with a light breeze. The weather forecast for Cortez predicted possible rain or snow in the late afternoon. We arrived an hour early and the chairs were already filling up under the large green & white striped awning placed by the gravesite. Introductions quietly made, as the various veterans groups and other dignitaries arrived. The last minute changes were hurriedly discussed as the starting time moved closer. I was still apprehensive about the outcome of the event and the wide variety of arrangements that had been made by so many people. This would not be the orchestrated ceremony as the military presents at Arlington National Cemetery. Instead it would be a small town honoring one of its own with their best efforts.

The Cortez cemetery was old, many generations were buried there, yet it was very plain and simple in design. The cemetery had winding paths with narrow roads between the plot sections. There were still a few stubborn clumps of snow tucked under some of the hedges. However, the Veteran's Section where John Spruell would have his gravestone had only recently opened and most of the surrounding plots were unused and there was very little vegetation in the area. Landscaping was minimal and the natural meadow grass had been mowed around the area where the Ceremony would take place. Thankfully, due to the recent snow and rain there was little dust despite the sudden vehicle and foot traffic.

More folks were arriving every minute. Fortunately additional chairs were available and were quickly & quietly being placed in lines under the awning and around the area as we prepared to start the Memorial Ceremony. Retired Master Chief Chaplain Leonard stepped up to the podium to do the introductions and Invocation. The various wreaths were presented and set up for display. More people kept showing up! Suddenly I realized that all of the seats were full and people were now standing in the back and even along the sides.

The front row seats were reserved for the Spruell family and friends. I sat on the left end of the front row, four seats from Dennis Spruell. Unexpectedly, I had the feeling of embarrassment and apprehension, as if I was an intruder on a very private moment. Carefully turning in my seat and looking around at the audience as the Chaplain was speaking I felt rather insignificant. It was an impressive sight, such a large gathering for an unknown person! Only a handful of people were still alive that had known John, none of them even remotely related to him. Yet John Spruell was now being honored as though each person present had known him. This had to be something special for Dennis Spruell and his family!

Finally, it was my turn to present the Eulogy. At one time a good public speaker, suddenly I was nervous and hesitant! Walking up to the podium and looking at all of the people assembled gave me a chill. I sure could use a cup of coffee right now! Surprisingly, someone handed me a Styrofoam cup of warm coffee as I was arranging the papers on the podium and looking at the expectant faces of the crowd, wondering if I had over obligated myself. I had written out an easy to read version of the Eulogy to use at the podium and printed up a fancy version to give to the Spruell family and the special guests in attendance. Shifting my cane to a more secure spot, taking a sip of coffee, I took a deep breath. Was I ready for this?

"Good morning ladies and gentlemen. Members of the Spruell family, honored guests, members of the military & veteran's organizations and especially members of the Chosin Few Association. As of today, Cortez has two National War Heroes from the Korean War, CPL John Spruell was one, and his high school friend A1C Jimmie Hobday is the other. Their names are inscribed on two of our National Monuments. As time passes, children grow up and society changes, we often forget about those around us who have done heroic deeds in the past. Especially if they have passed away and there are no family members to pass on their legacy. John Spruell died on 6 December 1950 and today marks 58 years since his death near the village of Hagaru-ri, on the side of a North Korean Reservoir called Chosin. The history books have not mentioned very much about this but now they are beginning to acknowledge that the battle around the Chosin Reservoir was one of the worst military disasters in our recent history.

Allied forces were sent to Korea by the United Nations because of Chinese & Russian assistance to a bunch of Korean rebels and the fact that China & Russia were slowly slipping into that small country their best Divisions of seasoned soldiers. This was the exact situation General MacArthur described when he warned President Truman about China & Russia, and was fired for it! That conflict became the Korean War, though the United Nations called it a "Police Action." A peace agreement and cease fire has never been formally signed, so technically this war is still going on today!

If you would, imagine a deep valley surrounded by high-mountain passes, the only access were roads that around here we would call burro trails. Quite often, having to be widened before the military could get their equipment through, or even to build a bridge across a river. The Allied forces did not know they were being led into a trap. Large Divisions of Chinese and Korean troops were waiting for them, and slowly surrounding this particular mountain range as the UN forces advanced.

The UN forces were being led, one small fight at a time into a giant bear trap. On 2 November 1950 the Chinese Army engaged the American 1st Marine Division suffering heavy casualties so when they retreated on the 6th of November the decision was made to lure the UN forces into a trap at the Chosin Reservoir. In an attempt to stop the repeated attacks by the Chinese, General MacArthur ordered the Army X Corps to attack the Chinese from the west of Chosin. As a result the X Corps was stretched out over a 400 mile line of convoys. The Allied commanders did not know the Chinese were being supplied with Russian intelligence as to the movement of US troops. Additional Divisions of Chinese troops were secretly sent into the Chosin Reservoir area beginning on the tenth of November.

As the American soldiers trudged through ever-increasing snow & cold, artillery would fire down upon their convoys and snipers would pick off troops. There were land mines, mountain slides, and other man made devices that would disable or stop their progress. Slowly the different Commands and Companies of the 7th Division and other military forces began to be cut-off from each other.

Enemy snipers would carefully begin to pick off the Officers, communications, and supply vehicles. Radio communication was poor or non-existent, food and supplies became more infrequent. The weather became worse and food that was served hot to the soldiers would often start to freeze before it could be eaten. Sometimes men froze to death in their sleep or while they just rested alongside the road. Our soldiers were ill prepared for the climate and the type of combat they now faced.

The Field Artillery Battalion that John Spruell was assigned to did not have it easy as they headed into the mountains. Sporadic attacks day and night, kept them awake. On the 26th of November 1950, during the night, the Chinese started to surround the entire 57th Field Artillery Battalion. They became engaged in a series of running battles over the next four nights that were so fierce that in just four days, the Battalion did not have any more ammunition for their 105MM Howitzer Cannons and they were running out of all their supplies. Several attacks by the Chinese were repulsed by the 57th FA Battalion by using their anti-aircraft guns against the ground troops. The provisional Regimental Combat Team (RCT) that had been created attempted on 28 &29 November to launch armored assaults on the Chinese only to fail because of slippery roads and inadequate infantry support.

American soldiers had to sabotage or abandon their equipment as they were being overrun by the Chinese and Korean soldiers. Most of the Command Chain had been killed off very quickly. Only a few Officers remained that were not severely injured. There was little or no communication with other military units. The Officers discovering too late, that they were being divided and worn down by 24 hour non-stop fighting so that the soldiers could no longer function properly. The temperature never got above 20 degrees during the day and would often drop as low as minus 30 degrees at night. By midnight of 30 November the remaining portion of the RCT & the 57th FA were facing four full Chinese regiments. The 57th repulsed another attack however their supply of ammunition for the anti-aircraft guns was almost gone.

On the First of December the remaining Officers disbanded the Artillery Battalion and led the troops down into the valley. Joining other fragmented units in an attempt to fight their way down into the Hagaru-ri valley where there was a large group of US Marines and what they thought would be safety. Some of the soldiers had already fought for eight days without sleep and had very little food. Many of the infantry soldiers were trapped on the east side of the Reservoir and the Marines were on the west side. Just over 100 men out of the Artillery Battalion made it into the Hagaru-ri valley by the 5th of December, a few more hundred men from the combined units, by the sixth.

Many of the surviving men from John Spruell's Battalion ended up trapped on the opposite side of the frozen reservoir. Some tried to cross the ice, most did not survive. The 5th & 6th of December were two of the worst days of the battle. There was no retreat, no supplies, and no help coming! A Detachment of Marines, sent into the valley to carve out a landing strip and to set up an Aid Station, slowly became the last line of defense for many of the soldiers.

Allied troops continued to flow into the valley, fighting their way through constant harassment, land mines, booby traps, and snipers. The trap was closing fast! Eventually, those that could be, were airlifted out by small planes, the largest being the military version of the DC-3 called a C-47. Though hundreds were saved many troops were left behind to die, as they were too seriously wounded or unable to reach the safety of the airfield. The remaining soldiers that eventually made it to the airfield or other emplacements on foot would somehow have to fight their way out of this valley or die trying.

Corporal John Spruell made it all the way down that mountain pass. He survived fighting in which his artillery battalion was decimated by ambush, severe winter weather that froze the rifles and cannon, improper clothing and scarce food. John died on 6 December 1950, somewhere near the village of Hagaru-ri by the Chosin Reservoir. I have talked with some of the survivors of that battle, I am sure that all of them will agree I have understated the reality of the situation and the conditions which they had to survive. However, they did survive! Those men are now proudly called the Chosin Few. Amongst every branch of the United States Military, they are honored and revered.

One of the men I have spoken to prior to the ceremony described to me his situation on 6 December. He was a Navy Corpsman (medic) at the Aid Station; the 5th Marine Detachment was protecting it. He remembers the day well. He thought that he was going to die before the day was out and was praying as he worked on the wounded. Snipers were shooting directly into the Aid Station area, killing the medical teams as well as the wounded they were trying to help. He was very scared but he continued to work trying to save the wounded.

Another Marine, Frank Brown, from D Company, 1st Marine Division also shared that terrible day as his birthday. " . . . I was just a grunt radio operator . . . We scraped out the "air strip" at Hagaru and we all have General O.P Smith's guidance to thank for most of us getting out of there alive. We started to fight our way out on Dec 6th, 1950, my 20th birthday and I really never thought I would see 21. I saw a quote recently that sort of rang true about us. "I wasn't a hero, but I was among heroes." Frank Brown, USMC.

The remaining forces fought their way out of that valley, inch by inch. Depending on the source, there is no true count of how many soldiers died, but less than five hundred men walked out of that valley at the end of the battle. Estimates in the low range over the two months that this battle went on are 2,500 men killed. 5,000 more wounded, 7,500 frostbite deaths and a minimum of 192 or more men are still unaccounted for and classed as missing. The remains of at least one thousand American and South Korean soldiers are still buried at the base of a hill just a few miles north of the Chosin Reservoir.

Corporal John Spruell is a Hero in his own right, for having fought and stayed alive through some of the most terrible conditions possible. The thought keeps running through my head that we should never forget his sacrifice or the lives of his fellow soldiers sacrificed from the Korean War or any other conflict, past, present or future.

War is a terrible thing and the men and women who willingly go into harms' way to protect others, should always be remembered. They should always be honored as heroes! To have made it through that kind of hellish fighting and weather John Spruell must have been one tough man. That is why we are here today to honor and remember Corporal John Spruell, 58 years after his death. He does not deserve to be forgotten any longer!"

After a brief pause to catch my breath, slowly turning to face the gravestone for John Spruell, I gave a crisp salute. Gathering my papers and my cane I returned to my seat. The Honor Guard slowly folded the United States flag and solemnly presented it to Dennis Spruell as the Rifle Squad prepared to give the twenty-one gun salute. SGT Burgess, standing behind the Rifle Squad, played TAPS and MC Leonard returned to the podium to thank everyone and close the Ceremony.

The Memorial Ceremony concluded, a reporter from the Cortez Journal came up to me with a smile on his face. Shaking my hand he said that after listening to everyone speak, the large turnout for this event, it should have had more of a write up in their paper, and that he would try to correct that with his story. I thanked him for his comments, hoping he would keep his word. A long line of cars clogged the small lanes of the cemetery as Chuck & Marilyn ushered me towards their car. We picked up Buzz from the veterinarian on our way to attend a by-invitation only lunch and a family meeting being held at the Spruell residence.

*   *   *PRESS*   *   *RELEASE*   *   *

"One of the Chosin Forgotten from the Korean War was finally remembered and honored after 58 years. Cortez, Colorado, 6 Dec 2008. POC: SFC Dane Hays, US Army Ret. Text Credits: Dane Hays & Steve Grazier (Cortez Journal Newspaper) Permission is granted to shorten the text as needed for publication.

*   *   *PRESS*   *   *RELEASE*   *   *

On 6 December 2008, a Memorial Ceremony took place at the Cortez Cemetery in Cortez, Colorado at 1PM, for Army Cpl. John A. Spruell, Battery B, 57th FA BN, 7th Infantry Division; he had been killed on 6 Dec 1950 in the Hagaru-ri Valley of the Chosin Reservoir in North Korea. His body was never recovered. The weather was slightly cool, 52 degrees, with a slight breeze. A large tent with chairs had been set up next to the gravesite. The Memorial Gravestone placed earlier in the week. Members of several Veterans' Organizations arrived early and so did the National Guard Honors Team sent by Governor Ritter of Colorado.

Several large wreaths and many smaller ones were placed to the side or around the gravesite, in addition to a personal wreath sent by Colorado Governor Ritter. As the family and local townsfolk began to take their seats under the canopy, it soon became evident that it would be standing room only. Representatives of over 36 Veterans Organizations stood by the side of the two Color Guards, one from the local Civil Air Patrol and the other from the American Legion Post. Eventually everyone had to form a half circle around the podium because of so many representatives arriving. The Honor Guard stood in the center, next to the podium, with the Rifle Team, quietly seated a short distance behind. This Memorial Ceremony, long in planning, took place on the 58th Anniversary of Cpl. Spruell's death. His records had been marked in error shortly after his death. The Spruell family had just recently been able to have the military records corrected.

The Memorial Ceremony started with a brief overview of Cpl. John Spruell's life & a prayer by Retired Marine Corps Chaplain Leonard. Next, the personal wreath from Governor Ritter was placed over the gravestone. Then a fellow high school classmate of John Spruell's, himself a Korean War Veteran, Chuck Haley with comments about their childhood together. The main Eulogy, presented by Retired Army SFC Dane Hays, whose father had grown up with Cpl. Spruell & was also a MIA/KIA in Korea. The Eulogy gave credit to the Chosin Few & the many Veteran's Organizations present. Then an overview of the Chosin Reservoir battle during November & December of 1950 with credit given to the 1st & 5th Marines for their support during the battle, for without them there would be no survivors. SFC Hays' last phrase, ending with a salute to the grave: "Cpl. John Spruell does not deserve to be forgotten any longer."

A Memorial Fund in the name of Cpl. John A. Spruell was established by two anonymous donors with the Cortez, Colorado Cemetery. The fund will provide for the upkeep, repair, & maintenance of the graves & headstones in the Veteran's Section of the cemetery in addition to providing financial relief to any family that cannot afford the cost of burying a family member that was a Veteran. The family has received over 50 letters from members of The Chosin Few, many more from veterans and Veteran's Organizations. The Mississippi Chapter of the 1st Marine Division Chosin Few has made Cpl. Spruell an Honorary Member & sent a bronze plaque now attached to his gravestone. The Commander, Disabled American Veterans Hawaii Division, sent a photo of the National MIA Memorial with an insert photo of Cpl. Spruell's marble plaque to the family."

Author's Note: Though there are too many to list, credit must be given to the numerous organizations and individuals who participated or made this Ceremony possible. I cannot take credit for all of the work nor should I attempt to do so. However, some must be recognized here out of courtesy and as a thank you for their efforts. Dennis Spruell & his family along with the VFW & American Legion chapters in Cortez did an amazing amount of work in a short time. Others deserving recognition are: Colorado Governor Ritter & his Homeland Security Staff; Chosen Few Association HQ (Don Gee); 1st Marine Division Chosin Few; Mississippi, Georgia & Missouri Chapters of The Chosin Few; The Army Chapter of The Chosin Few; 5th Marine Regt, 1st BN (Korea); Phoenix, AZ Chapter of AUSA, Denver, CO Chapter of AUSA, especially Rance Farrell, Paul Baldwin & Amy Weichel; George Rasula; John McLean of the 1st Cav. US Army; Bruce Salisbury, Jim Westendorf, Frank Brown & Charles Shaw. Without their help, intervention or guidance, this Memorial Ceremony for Corporal John Spruell would not have been possible.

-THE NEXT MORNING-

Waking up early and taking Buzz outside in the cold crisp air we found there was a light coating of ice on the back steps of Chuck's house. The grass was coated with a heavy layer of frost. Tiny footprints in the snow drifts along the back fence revealed where the deer, jumping the low wooden fence, had come into the yard looking for food. Chuck handed me a hot cup of coffee as Buzz & I came back into the house. Both of us expressed a sense of relief that the Memorial Ceremony was over. We marveled that there had been such a large turnout contrary to what the local newspaper had predicted or expected.

Marilyn cooked bacon & eggs while I hurriedly packed my bag. Buzz curled up by the fireplace, keeping an eye on the activity. We headed for the airport, still talking about all of the events that had occurred in the last few months. Chuck and Marilyn were fine people and so were all the other folks I had been introduced to during my stay in Cortez. I was leaving Cortez with some very special memories, new friends, and a different perspective on life. Yet I could not shake the odd feeling as I boarded the airplane that I had left Cortez with unfinished business. Someday I would return to visit. It would be a nice place to live.

The flight home was one of mixed feelings. I was elated that the Spruell Memorial Ceremony had been such a success and that I had made some new friends, discovered a previously unknown family connection, and very relieved that the Ceremony was over. Cortez felt like 'home 'and now I had a connection with the town and people that would never be broken. Becky, the cemetery director had suggested that I could reserve the empty plot next to John Spruell for myself. That left a big lump sticking in my throat! I would be honored to have my ashes placed next to John Spruell's gravestone!

However, there was bad news also which threatened to make this a sad occasion. The Cortez veterinarian said Buzz had a tumor on his hip. An operation may or may not save his life, as there was no way to know what damage had been done to him internally. She gave me a typed medical report and several x-rays to show my veterinarian in Sedona. I needed to make some tough decisions when I returned to the nursing home in Sedona! Decisions that could cost Buzz his life! There was a lot to think about as the small plane began to gain altitude as it left Cortez, passing by the snowcapped mountains below.

-RETURNING TO SEDONA-

Upon arrival at Sky Harbor International Airport in Phoenix later that afternoon Buzz & I quickly boarded the shuttle bus back to the nursing home in Sedona. I was tired and physically exhausted yet energized by all that had happened. I noticed that Buzz was limping a bit. He had trouble standing still, something was definitely wrong! After a days' rest, I began the tedious process of putting all of my notes together and processing the photos stored in my digital camera.

I had gone to Cortez a stranger, to participate in a Memorial Ceremony for a stranger, and returned feeling that I had gained a family and friends. Chuck and his wife Marilyn had been gracious hosts and in the process became sincere friends. They talked about Jimmie, their childhood days in Cortez, making me feel like I was a friend just returned from a trip. Dennis Spruell and his family were honest hard working folks that were eager to learn about a part of the family history previously unknown to them. Dennis was working in local law enforcement as an undercover officer and considering running for Sheriff in another year or two. Cortez was a sleepy little town that had suddenly become my adopted home. The trip was an absolute success thanks to the help and hard work of so many strangers! Yet it was still difficult for me to acknowledge that Jimmie Hobday was my birth father in casual conversation!

CHAPTER SEVENTEEN

The local veterinarian in Sedona, Doctor Post, was not able to see Buzz until four days after we returned from Cortez. The taxi ride from the nursing home took less than ten minutes but it felt like an hour's drive. Dr. Post looked at the x-rays I had brought back from Cortez and made a thorough examination. He agreed that Buzz had a tumor but did not feel it was as serious as the Cortez veterinarian had stated. However, Doctor Post said there were three lumps instead of one, two of them in his abdomen, and that we should take at least one of them out now and wait to see how Buzz does after that. Because of his status as a Service Dog, I kept pet insurance on Buzz, which would cover part of the costs but not all. This would be a very expensive operation. Accepting the need for expediency I gave Buzz a hug and returned to the nursing home alone, with tearful eyes. I barely slept that night, worrying about Buzz. Dr. Post operated on him early the next morning; I was so upset I could not eat dinner that night or breakfast the next morning.

True to his nature, Buzz took the surgery in stride maintaining his upbeat personality. I arrived at the clinic shortly after breakfast as Buzz was waking up. He was sore and groggy but perky in spirit as I placed him on the seat of the taxi for the return trip to the nursing home. His bandage would have to be changed each day and the pain tablets would make him a bit groggy. He wagged his tail and watched me intently as we sat in the taxi.

After a couple of days Buzz perked up and began to act as if everything was okay. Then I noticed about a week later that Buzz was not his usual energetic attentive self and he was again starting to walk slower. Determined to be close to me, despite great pain, his strength was failing. At first, thinking it was just a reaction to the surgery, I just tried to comfort him but something did not seem right so I began to make notes and take pictures. When I phoned Doctor Post that Friday and described the situation, he said it was probably part of the healing process. Not to worry, just give Buzz a little more time to heal.

Less than three weeks after the surgery, Buzz was lying on his bed with a glassy eyed look and having trouble breathing. Trying to stand and eat was difficult; he was beginning to lose weight, as he would only eat a small amount of food. Buzz was rapidly becoming very lethargic, his shiny coat seemed to dull and age overnight. Over the next few days, his conditioned worsened and one morning I had to carry him outside so he could do his business, as he could not walk. We made another trip to the veterinarian's office that morning.

After a twenty-minute exam, Doctor Post came into the lobby to talk. The surgery had healed without problem but that was not the cause of Buzz's discomfort. There were several more smaller rapidly growing tumors with one large tumor growing inside his abdomen. They were like mushrooms, sprouting up overnight! The tumors were starting to interfere with his vital organs and bodily processes. More surgery would be dangerous and very expensive with no guarantee of success. After all, Buzz was ten years old, had led a very active life and this might just be part of his aging process. Doctor Post urged me to take Buzz home and think about the situation for a day or two before making a final decision.

Buzz continued to worsen! He could barely stand and spent all of his time lying on his bed and sometimes you could hear his labored breathing mixed with a whimper. Three days later, I called the vet and told him I was bringing Buzz back to the clinic. Upon our arrival at the clinic Wednesday morning, Doctor Post met us at the door. He took one look at Buzz and shook his head. "I thought you might be over reacting but I see now you are right, it is time to ease his misery."

Doctor Post led me to a small room as I gently cradled Buzz in my arms. Carefully placing Buzz on the stainless steel table, I tried to comfort him. As Dr. Post prepared the syringe he tried to reassure me that I had done everything possible for Buzz. Buzz looked up at me as though to say thanks for a good life while I stroked his head. Trying very hard to hold back the tears in my eyes as I spoke to him, Buzz died peacefully in my arms that morning without a whimper.

Stepping into the taxi to return to the nursing home without Buzz, I could not hold the tears back any longer. Taking my meals in my room and avoiding everyone, I cried for two days. Thursday I returned to the clinic to pick up the small cedar box that held Buzz's ashes. Depressed and sad over Buzz I kept busy by working on the notes and pictures from the Spruell Memorial Ceremony. Eyes filled with tears every time I thought about him or if I looked at one of his pictures.

Buzz had been companion, friend, and helper for ten years; I would not forget him easily! That dog had gone everywhere with me, even to doctor's appointments, always with his quiet and well-behaved manner. His ability to sense my medical needs had been uncanny at times yet Buzz had always maintained an energetic and upbeat personality. For many years, if I was threatened or there was an emergency I had wondered how Buzz would react. When I had my first heart attack in November of 2003 and was unable to move, Buzz had stayed by my side, keeping me awake and warm until I could get up and obtain medical care.

His devotion and protectiveness came into full play several months later when we were in Quartzsite, Arizona. The two of us had gone out in the desert on the ATV Gator for our daily exercise. Stopping to let him run and explore a bit while I stood next to the ATV I noticed a clump of sage brush at the edge of a small ravine start to rustle. I had unknowingly parked next to a ravine where an injured female coyote was hiding. Buzz was off to one side, following a rabbit trail when the coyote leaped out of the bushes, her jaws wide open and aimed for my throat. Before the coyote could reach me, Buzz came from behind at a run, catching her throat in mid-air and snapping her neck with one twist. Watching the coyote and looking back to see if I was okay he stood vigilantly between us. After that, I never questioned his ability or loyalty! I knew Buzz was a special dog!

One year later, I was having dinner at a restaurant in Lake Havasu when I started to have a seizure. Buzz began pulling on my pant leg just before the seizure began trying to get my attention. As we were departing the restaurant, the seizure caused me to lose control of the electric mobility chair for a moment. I knew I was in trouble! It was 9p.m. and a dark summer night in a part of town with little traffic. The restaurant manager had locked the door as we left. It was closing time and there was no one left in the parking lot. I did not have a cell phone and no one heard my feeble cries for assistance. All I could do was hope for the best until I could get home or find help. Putting the chair in neutral, I told Buzz to take me home. Buzz pulled that one hundred pound electric chair over three miles, navigating sidewalks, and intersections! As we neared the house, strength began to return to my arms and I was able to regain control of the chair. Yes, Buzz was special! To replace a dog like that would be impossible!

I found a new obsession for a while that helped in the grieving process. The story of Buzz was sent out on the internet to everyone I knew. Knowing that his companionship had been one of the primary reasons for my recovery from the military injuries and an enjoyable life over the last ten years, I immediately began to search for another dog.

Obviously, I could not afford to pay the thousands of dollars for another school-trained dog and I was in no position in the nursing home to take care of a puppy either. In addition, I learned that without a dog I would have to move into a shared room with one of the other nursing home residents. Which I did not want to do unless it was absolutely necessary! Researching the internet, I discovered several agencies that would donate trained dogs to disabled veterans, but most of them had a long waiting list or lengthy application process.

Another route to consider was the adoption of a retired Military War Dog from the government. Retired Military War Dogs were given a chance at a new life if they could pass a series of tests to prove they were not dangerous to the public. The prospective owner also had to meet certain standards before a dog was given to them. I spent many hours completing applications for the various agencies and programs, hoping that one of them might be willing to cut down the waiting time. Finally I was given approval to receive a War Dog and started a serious search for the right one. However, there were other concerns that required immediate attention! My life was changing again!

CHAPTER EIGHTEEN

ANOTHER NIGHT OF WAKING UP IN EXCRUTIATING PAIN!

SEDONA—29 DECEMBER 2008

The third time in one week! The angina is back! The first time I calmly suffered through it. Then when the second time occurred, taking one Nitro tablet the pain went away. I thought it was just my imagination and ignored it. This time I recorded my blood pressure (190/95) and took two Nitro tabs. The pain eased right away. Maybe it's nothing, but I am afraid my heart is giving me trouble again, possibly another blockage. It was three weeks since I was in Cortez, I cannot tell the doctor, as he would probably cancel any future trips because of a possible heart attack. This book must be finished and I have to complete all of the plans that have been set in motion. Even if it kills me in the process! It could just be something as simple as the stress of the trip and worry over Buzz.

I'll start keeping a record of my blood pressure and making notes on any future attacks so that I would have something to show the doctor. Then a few days later I remembered what the Neurologist Doctor Pavi had said about one of the medications, Tizanidine. I was one of the rare people that could build up a toxic level of the medication in their body which would then mimic an angina attack. It could even make it appear that you were having a stroke! I had already gone to the Emergency Room once because of this and that had been diagnosed as the cause for that trip. Calling Doctor Pavi the next morning, discussing the problems and asking her if we could reduce the dosage, she agreed. It worked! There was no more pain or problems!

Maybe that is why all of my nightmares, my PTSD dreams, end with my death! Somebody upstairs is trying to tell me something! Well I am a stubborn old man! I'm going to see this through, I may just have to adjust a few things and make some early preparations. I will make the trip to Arlington National Cemetery to see Jimmie's headstone put in place. Sometime, I will have to go back to Cortez and make sure that all of the preparations are complete for my own burial next to John Spruell. Arrangements will be made so that Jimmie & his fellow crewmembers will be properly honored, even after my death. The first thing I must do is draw up a set of Codicils to my Will, making the changes that can put everything into motion no matter what happens to me.

Someone else may have to write the last chapter if I don't finish this book! A feeling of absolute urgency overwhelms me at times, wanting to accomplish so much in such a short amount of time. For whatever reason, I feel that this saga must be told! My life won't have been in vain, or that of my birth father, Jimmie Hobday, and his fellow crewmembers in that B-29.

It would be so much easier if Joan/Sister Jose would give me the chance to talk with her in person. I keep looking every day in the mail for the envelope that Fred Parker had promised he was going to mail. Fred said he was including information about their life at Kadena AFB and even a bit about that terrible night in September

1952 over North Korea. So much to accomplish and there may not be enough time! I was still extremely fragile medically and might possibly require assisted living for the rest of my life.

The year spent as a Prisoner Of War in Korea had given Fred Parker too many painful nightmares and memories. Adding to that, he has had a bad case of pneumonia for several months. Fred cannot drive an automobile anymore yet he will push himself to exhaustion with his farm equipment. When talking to Fred on the phone, you can hear his lungs rattle like a tin can full of marbles. Perhaps, remembering Jimmie is just too much for him on top of everything else. I could not guess or imagine the horrors and suffering that Fred and his fellow captors endured when they were prisoners.

Just a few days after that severe angina attack, in the midst of mailing out the last of the news releases & photos on the Spruell ceremony, I received a large brown mailer envelope. It was from Fred Parker! He had written a wonderful two-page letter in small, hesitant, very shaky handwriting. Fred included fifteen pictures of fellow crewmembers along with some of dad. He had labeled each one on the back and several were marked with "This is your dad." That just sent chills down my back! Fred had done the very thing I wished for but had been afraid to ask. Now, in a sense, I had someone else acknowledging that Jimmie Hobday was my dad! Copying the photos from Fred, then adding two of my own photos, one taken prior to my retirement, the other, recently taken at the nursing home I began to compare the facial features.

The first photo most likely taken at the baseball field at Kadena, Jimmie had lost a lot of weight. A second photo showed Jimmie in a flight suit; it was obvious he was getting thinner. Then the third was at the door of the barracks tent. Dad had toned up his muscles but taken on a battle-hardened face. Jimmie looked tired, worn out, and they had only been in Korea four months. Another photo showed part of the crew standing in front of the tent, dad had a cigarette in his mouth that he was trying to remove. There was also a picture of

Fred Parker on the troop ship headed home after his release from the POW Camp in 1953.

Comparing my thinner face at age 42 and the fuller face at age 61 against the photos of Jimmie and noting the differences. So many similarities and differences! Other than my mother's jaw and the paler skin tone, we looked very much alike. As a test, I lined up a bunch of military photos, mixed a couple of mine in, and showed them around to the staff of the nursing home. Everyone picked Jimmie out, especially the one of him standing at the entrance to the tent and said, "That is your dad isn't it?" No one missed seeing the resemblance! It felt so re-assuring and yet brought tears to my eyes every time I looked at the photos. The photo at the tent door was most likely taken shortly before Jimmie died on that bombing mission. He had lost a lot of weight and looked pale. More like a gaunt stranger in comparison to his photographs from just a few years before. The amount of stress those men felt each time they took off on another bombing mission must have been tremendous! It took courage and dedication to fly those missions knowing that you might never come back from the next run.

I re-read Fred Parker's letter several times, looking at each photograph carefully. It must have been painful for Fred to dredge up some of those old memories. One could almost feel the pain as Fred wrote the letter. His hands would have been shaking as he placed the photographs into that little envelope. I don't think Fred will ever know how much his letter and those photos meant to me. He had endured and survived an ordeal many career military men dread. One can only imagine his suffering and the resulting pains & nightmares that would plague him for the rest of his life. I wanted to meet Fred Parker in person but realized that such an event was just about impossible. Perhaps there would be a chance sometime in the future. Bud Farrell has said that he would stay in contact with Fred and maybe have a chance to visit him sometime in the future.

Dear Dave

Trying to recall things that happened 55 years ago is a big assignment for me but Parhops I might mention a few of the things we did as a crew.

these are in no particular order but here are some of the high lights. on a training mission it was about 14 hr long we were heading back to base and most of the Crew Wer asleep unbuckles we hit an air pocket and dropid about 500 feet. I happened to be buckeled up and was ok. but every one else Came out of there seats. it was funny.

on One mission we flew With out the Aut power working so on the way up to taaget we iced up and Used up more fuel so we were forced to fly into Japan. it was a short run way and we had to use our Hydraulic breaks, but they depended on our A.P.U. to keep the hudraulic pumped up. so we had to hit the run way with tho breaks locked blew out two or three tires. well we made the landing ok but had to have tire flown so we had about five days vacation in Japan. That was fun.

One of the things we enjoyed at the end of a bomb run. We usually got back to base early in the morning so breakfast was the first order of the day and we all ways had fresh eggs and fresh milk. I'm sure you know by now Jimmie's position was tail gunner so he was isolated from the crew from beginning to end of a mission. Jimmie was a happy go lucky kind of a guy and got along with every one. He was hard to wake up in the morning so we litterly had to drag him out of bed for breakfast.

Dane I am sending several photos and a copy of the award for you to keep. Perhaps with time I'll remember more. I hope these will be of some comfort to you.

your good friend
Fred Parker Jr
Wishing you a
merry Christmas

On the evening of 17 January 2009 a set of emails arrived that left me anxiously waiting for more news. I had posted an inquiry on a website called The Korean War Project run by Ted Barker, looking for more information on the bomber crews. A gentleman by the name of Bill "Ezzra" Aseere replied to one of the postings.

"I lived in the tent next to Royer's crew. Captain William C. Campbell was my pilot. I was the tail gunner. I flew the same mission the night we lost them. After the mission, instead of hell raising and playing in the tent, it was dark and quiet! I don't remember their names but I remember their faces." I hastily sent Bill Aseere an email reply:

"Hi Ezzra, My name is Dane Hobday Hays, US Army Retired. My birth father was the tail gunner in LT Royer's crew, AIC Jimmie Hobday of Cortez, Colorado. If you were in that tent next to them, I bet you knew my dad. I know he was a bit of a loner and hung around with another member of his crew that was a loner also, Fred Parker. I have included a photo of me, and the crew photo from Randolph AFB.

Do you remember him? Would you have any photos of him or other members of the crew? If you remember my dad Jimmie, would you mind talking about him a bit? I only knew him for the first 2 ¾ years of my life, but heard his name all through my childhood. Then I found a whole stack of photos and letters that my mother had kept hidden for over 65 years. So I am searching for anyone that might have known him."

Bill Aseere must have been on his computer at the same time because his reply came back within a few minutes.

"Dane, Yes I knew your father. We all played cards together almost every day. He was a quiet and calm guy. We were both tail gunners so we had a lot to talk about after every mission. I don't remember how many missions they flew until that night. We ended up with 31. I saw the plane blow up! We were just ahead. They never knew what hit them.

Also I remember that night as our radar man (LT. Gates) painted one too many aircraft in our stream, then shortly before the Flak started, one of the blips left the stream. Later we found out the extra blip on the radar was a TU-4, a Russian copy of a B-29 that was downed in North Korea sometime before. The probability was it was reporting our airspeed and altitude to the Flak batteries below. That is why we caught so much hell that night. The Flak was very accurate that night compared to the barrage type we usually experienced.

I am now 75 years old, playing golf and enjoying retirement in Florida. There isn't a day I don't think of those guys and many others that never got a chance to live a full life and wonder why I was allowed to. The right gunner and myself are the only ones from our crew still alive. Nice to hear from you and to let you know your father was a fine man. Regards, William "Ezzra" Aseeere."

Within a short amount of time I had found three individuals that were directly connected to Jimmie Hobday and the fatal bombing mission over Suiho, Korea! Contrary to my earlier feelings of desperation, I was beginning to feel that maybe it was not too late. Perhaps at this late date more revelations were still to come. Against all odds, people were still alive that were connected to Jimmie Hobday and John Spruell in some manner. This endeavor would require a lot more time and effort. I would have to continue my research and be prepared for more unexpected results and surprises.

CHAPTER NINETEEN

PRESCOTT VALLEY, ARIZONA—JANUARY 2009

The Veterans Administration will take care of my Headstone when I die, shipping it to the cemetery at Cortez. All I have to do is set up a way for the burial plot or cemetery fees to be paid for when I die and complete a few forms for them to keep on file. The cemetery had already placed a small marker next to John Spruell's gravestone to mark my final resting place. One thing more had to be done, there had to be some type of memorial plaque that would honor Jimmie and his fellow crewmembers.

Designing a memorial plaque was not as easy as I had thought it would be, so after two days of fruitless effort I decided that was something better left to the professionals. To my surprise, only a couple of engraving companies in Arizona would take on small jobs. An engraving company in nearby Flagstaff said they would do the job if I would send them a note with the information and they would do the layout. Once they had come up with a design, it would be sent to me for approval before they did the actual casting.

A week later Flag Stamp & Engraving Company sent me a letter with four possible designs. I quickly called them with my choice and placed the order. The finished plaque would be mailed to me in about two weeks. I could not believe my eyes when the heavy 8 inch wide by 14 inch long bronze plaque arrived in the mail. It was perfect! The raised lettering offset by the dark rocky background made a striking combination. The bronze plaque had cost $325, and was worth every penny!

The difficult part would be arranging for the bronze memorial plaque to be delivered to the cemetery after my death and the attachment to the headstone. When I had called Becky at the Cortez cemetery and told her what I was planning, she liked the idea but did not feel it would be wise to have the plaque sitting around for a long time in the cemetery office as it could be lost or damaged. Arrangements would have to be made for it to be sent to the cemetery after I died. What an ironic twist! My cemetery plot would be next to John Spruell's and the bronze plaque, attached to my headstone would in a sense tie both men together once again.

DEDICATED TO THE
HONOR, LOVE & MEMORY
OF MY FATHER

A1C JIMMIE HOBDAY

AND HIS B29 CREWMEMBERS
SHOT DOWN OVER N. KOREA
ON 13 SEPT 1952

CPT LOWE   1LT BLOESCH
MSGT BROWN   1LT KELLY
A1C KELLY   1LT PETERS
A1C LeBARON   1LT PHILLIS
A1C TROSCLAIR   1LT ROYER

Only time and God can determine what will happen in the future, but I cannot allow this story to go untold. For many reasons it is too important! The rejection, abuse, and lack of love that I received as a child; the loss of heroes like Jimmie Hobday, John Spruell and the survivors of Chosin, all seemingly intertwined in the lives of many people still alive today. Possibly, by someone reading this story, it might save another child from going through the pain and nightmare that I lived as a child and all the doubts and fears that plagued my life as a result. Perhaps through this story other military members will not be so easily forgotten in future wars by their hometowns or family members.

Folks like the Spruell family should not have to go through half a century before they find out about a family member or loved one that has served honorably in the military in years past and died a forgotten hero. Sadly, if John Spruell's parents had not been afraid of ridicule and other folks in Cortez had been more understanding, life could have been better for them. By a twist of fate, the military records of Jimmie Hobday and John Spruell had been erroneously labeled only to be corrected many years later. What would have happened if those records had never been corrected?

Shortly after receiving Fred's letter, another shocking event occurred in my life. Upon further examination the Veteran's Administration doctors had concluded that the heart surgery I had seven months earlier to remove the 70% blockage was successful and that my body was slowly beginning to heal. In addition, the VA had adopted Dr. Nagy's suggested medication regimen which was proving to further aid my recuperation. I was no longer a "terminal case" and did not need to reside in a full care nursing home, but I still needed assistance. I might actually improve enough in time to live on my own again. However, for the immediate future I still needed some assistance and a light degree of medical management. Once more, the Veteran's Administration decided that I needed to move with a two-week notice!

The VA Hospital Social Worker, Steve Perkins, drove me around to interview and tour several assisted care facilities in the Prescott area. All of them would be closer to the VA Hospital so I would no longer have the one-hour drive from Sedona. Unfortunately, because of the improving health, the VA would no longer cover the assisted living costs, only the medications and treatments.

The first week of February 2009, I moved from Sedona to Grayson House, a clean & quiet upscale assisted care facility in Prescott Valley. Instead of 120 beds, this facility had forty private rooms with only about 30 residents. It was considerably nicer than the nursing home in Sedona, great food, a better atmosphere and I could even go to the local shopping center with my mobility chair. Best of all, I could have a dog in my room and it did not have to be a Service Dog!

The local Humane Society picked up the story about the loss of Buzz and the search for another dog. One of their workers, Dawn Gonzales, began bringing dogs over to the nursing home for me to consider adopting. I would keep each one for a couple of days to determine if they would be workable in the nursing home. After several failed attempts, I was losing hope of finding a replacement for Buzz. When I left the nursing home in Sedona, I had given all of the Service Dog gear and his beds to a local trainer/breeder, Fran Elliot, who specialized in service dogs for autistic children. As a result, I no longer had my training tools and accessories that could be used if I found a new dog so this one would have to have some natural abilities. Even Fran was encouraging me to find a new dog!

Dawn called me late one afternoon the first week of March. A small female dog had arrived at the Humane Shelter that morning. She was the same breed mix as Buzz, Border Collie & Australian Shepard, smaller in size and only about two or three years old. The dog had been abused, chained to a porch for two or more years No training of any sort yet she seemed to have a distinct personality and calmness. Would I be interested in working with the dog if they covered the cost of her adoption? I told Dawn that I would look at the dog but I did not know if I could handle an extensive training program while living in assisted care. Dawn said she could bring the dog out the next morning but please do not be put off by the dog's appearance as she needed a bath and haircut.

Shortly after breakfast the next day I sat on the front porch waiting. Dawn drove up and parked in front of me. She opened the back gate of her station wagon and there was a dog inside her travel kennel. Dirty and needing a haircut was a mild statement! The dog was an absolute mess! The black hair caked with mud, and grown so long it was dragging the ground more like that of an English sheep dog. Her nails, probably never cut, were so long they had curved under her feet so that she was actually walking on her nails. The dog had bug eggs in her ears and her muddied coat smelled terrible. Attaching a leash, I walked her around the parking lot next to my mobility chair. She did not shy away and even sat down when I stopped. Before I could take her inside, she would definitely have to have a bath and a haircut, maybe more. We agreed that I would work with her for a couple of days but if the dog turned out to be a problem, Dawn would pick her up immediately and return her to the shelter.

I spent the entire day bathing and trimming the dog, using the water hose at the back of the building. Since I could not take the dog inside until she was clean, the cook brought a lunch plate out to me so I could eat while working on the dog. The Hispanic name the original owners had given the dog, Pulgoso, was difficult for me to pronounce so I shortened it to Pooh, to which she readily responded. By dinnertime, Pooh was finally clean enough to take inside the building. Surmising that this had been the first time Pooh was ever bathed or trimmed; I was surprised that she took it so calmly.

Possibly, Pooh accepted the grooming as a form of attention and love that she had never had before. She was at least ten to fifteen pounds underweight and suffering from malnutrition which was easily corrected with proper diet and vitamin supplements. While cutting Pooh's hair that afternoon, I noticed a striking resemblance to Buzz! The basic breed mixture was the same but Buzz had been the smooth coated Border Collie & Pooh's ancestors had been the rough coated Border Collie.

Three days later, I called Dawn and told her I would like to keep Pooh. The dog did not bark or howl, she was very subdued, and yet very friendly when people came up to her. Pooh slept quietly at night on the pad I had placed next to the bed. During meal times at the nursing home I parked my mobility chair in the hallway with Pooh attached to it with a leash so she could watch me at the dining table. Pooh even handled going to the shopping mall without any problem when I used the folding walker. After several days of working with Pooh I concluded that with lots of love and training she would make a good companion and called Dawn Gonzales to give her the good news!

-TWO WEEKS LATER-

It is only the fifth of April and already 80 degrees at noon, perhaps this warming trend indicates a hot summer. The air conditioning within the assisted care home actually came on for a short time this afternoon. Just as I was getting ready to go down the hall for lunch, the phone rang. It was an automated call from the Catholic Diocese in Tucson. Sister Jose (Joan) Hobday quietly passed away this morning at the Catholic Hospice in Tucson.

Stunned and deeply saddened by the passing of such a talented, gentle woman, I managed to muddle through the meal in the dining room. I knew Sister Jose was seriously ill and that this time would eventually come, but still I was not prepared for it to be this soon. Coming back to my small room and pulling Pooh into my arms, I began to cry. Even though I had never met Joan/Sister Jose in person, we had shared so many phone calls and letters. Reading Sister Jose's inspirational books, then discussing them with her on the telephone had made it seem like we were old friends. I emailed the Diocese and found that the Memorial Mass would be in Tucson in two weeks. There was no way I could attend. Since they had an online guest registry for the service, I entered a short note of bereavement.

The Diocese sent an excerpt from the Bishop's Monday Memo regarding Sister Jose: "Please pray for the repose of the soul of

Sister Jose Hobday, O.S.F., who died Sunday. Sister Jose, who made Tucson her home, was a nationally known author & speaker on prayer and spirituality. A 2003 story in Canada's Western Catholic Reporter, headlined "Spirituality transcends culture," will tell you much about Sister Jose. Reporter Bill Glen wrote: "Christ set the example, says Sister Jose Hobday, of how we must recognize the special virtues within all of us, and disregards cultural differences. If, as Christians, we can remember the Kingdom of God is within us & all around us, then the difference we make doesn't have to be glorious or well know-even appreciated." She said, "The greatest influences in life don't always come from glitz and superstars. They come from the goodness of people."

"We pray Sister Jose will enjoy the Paschal celebration this year with the Lord. There will be a celebration of her life in a special Memorial Mass at Blessed Kateri Tekakwitha Parish in Tucson on Wednesday at 2pm."

The local newspapers had quite a write-up and the Diocese website even devoted two large articles concerning Sister Jose. I wondered if Bishop Kicanas remembered my letter and phone call about her and if he would be contacting me.

As I looked over my notes an article caught my eye, it was an excerpt from the book "A Woman's Path" written by Jo Giese about Sister Jose. "Sister Jo is just as likely to be found sharing the stage with the Dalai Lama in Chicago, speaking about simplicity and spirituality, or driving a Jeep in New Mexico, teaching the native people how to get the resources they need. Every five to seven years she's had a moment of clarity, her work has changed, and her path has led her somewhere new." What a wonderful woman Joan had become!

Two weeks after Sister Jose died; I received another unexpected phone call. This time it was from J.B.Wiles at the Air Force Casualty Office in the Pentagon. Sister Jose had appointed me her alternate representative to the Air Force, in case something happened and she was unable to fulfill the obligations. In all of our conversations, she had never said anything about doing this! The Memorial Ceremony had been delayed again due to her poor health. All this time I had assumed the Ceremony had taken place on schedule! Now that she had passed, they wanted to know if I planned to come to Arlington National Cemetery for the Memorial Ceremony, rescheduled for 23 July. WOW! Of course, I will be there!

-ARLINGTON BOUND-

It took six hours of shopping, laboriously comparing prices on the internet to find a set of flights that would get me to Arlington and back without great expense. I had spent four years living in Arlington, Virginia during the mid-1990s while working as a Veteran's Advocate and Lobbyist. My bedroom window had overlooked a portion of the Arlington National Cemetery and I had heard the rifle squads firing their salute and the bugle playing TAPS on a daily basis. I would be able to stay overnight in Denver on the return trip to rest up at a hotel before returning to Arizona. One connection had only ½ hour to change planes at the opposite end of the airport terminal, so I decided that taking my fold-up electric scooter could be a liability.

Because of recently increased airport security requirements and new luggage restrictions, I would have to travel with only a small overnight carry-on bag and the folding walker. Due to the nature of some of the medical equipment and medications that I required just to function, care had to be taken in packing the carry-on bag and making sure all of my medications were properly labeled. Not only did I have to take extra medications but also the prescription refill slips had to go also just in case of an emergency. Flight schedules had to allow for the time spent waiting in line for security screenings. Flying used to be so easy! One of the folks that visited Grayson House assisted care on a frequent basis volunteered to take care of Pooh for the few days I would be gone.

The little Great Lakes Airlines commuter plane from Prescott to Denver was delayed by an hour so I missed my original connection but was able to catch another flight from Denver that actually got me to Dulles International Airport in Virginia two hours earlier than planned. That allowed me time to sleep for three hours. Finding a quiet corner on the third floor, I stretched out on a couple of chairs and covered myself with my coat. I woke up about 6a.m. when the security officers were making their rounds. Grabbing a bite to eat at the food court on the first floor provided a much needed breakfast and coffee. Next would be the task of shaving and changing clothes. Luckily I found a handicapped restroom with a locking door nearby.

If the housekeeping woman had opened the door that morning, she would have had quite a shock. I stripped off my clothes, did a sponge bath, a quick shave, and then redressed putting on my dark suit for the Memorial Ceremony. Repacking was easy since I no longer had to worry about wrinkling the suit I had carefully kept folded inside the bag. Another tall cappuccino from the concession stand fortified me for a few hours.

Walking towards the street exit of the air terminal, I took a deep breath and squared my shoulders. Today was going to be special and I was not going to allow anything to spoil it! It was raining lightly as I left the terminal; the misty air was tainted by the odor of jet fuel and auto exhaust. That was okay, having lived there before and knowing the fickle weather; I had brought along an umbrella and a raincoat.

Once again, fortune smiled! I had saved the expired handicap ID and discount fare cards for the subway from when I had previously lived in Arlington. The subway system that covers the District of Columbia region extended into parts of Virginia and Maryland. It was rated as one of the best systems in the United States. Planning to go to the Metro Station Office to renew them before I went to Arlington National Cemetery, I had expected to pay full fare for part of the ride. However, when I boarded the bus outside the air terminal to take me to the subway station the driver said that I could still use the ID card and discounted fare cards since it was just for the one day. That kind act saved me quite a bit of time and money!

The rain stopped as I stepped off the bus and headed towards the entrance to the subway. The ten-year old discount card opened the turnstile without any problem. The ride was quick, another hour and the bus and subway would have been crowded with people going to work. Arriving an hour earlier than planned at Arlington National Cemetery, I found the wrought iron gated entrance still locked. My only choice was to quietly join the line of people already lining up to wait for the cemetery to open. Our footsteps left a hollow sound on the cobblestoned driveway in front of the gate. The high humidity was making me sweat under that dark suit so I tried to stay in the shade as much as possible.

My appointment with the Casualty Office & Mortuary Affairs representatives was not until 10am with the Memorial Ceremony starting at 11am sharp. I had two hours to kill. It had started to rain again as I sat down inside the lobby. Buying a cup of coffee from the nearby refreshment booth, an empty seat was found near the door that led to the offices. The next hour was spent watching the people pass by. Some people were very somber; several chatty individuals were obviously tourists. A group of local high school students being escorted for a tour was more interested in gossip than the many displays in the lobby. A few visitors were quietly chatting about the various displays in the lobby; others appeared to be lost in deep thought.

Rain had turned into a light mist and I was not interested in another cup of coffee so out of boredom I took the one-hour tram tour of the Cemetery. The tour guide noticed the military rank insignia on my carry-on bag and asked me what branch of service I had served with and why I was there. When I told her about Jimmie's Memorial Ceremony, she made it a point to welcome me when she started her tour story as the tram made its way through the narrow tree lined asphalt path. We arrived back at the entrance just in time for me to report in at the Casualty Office conference room. It had sprinkled off & on during the tram ride, now the sun was shining through again as the clouds began to lift. Glancing out the lobby window, I could see the asphalt pathways steaming as the sun began to warm them. I was glad to be inside with the air conditioning.

One of the Mortuary Affairs staff, a young Air Force sergeant by the name of Adams opened the office door and quickly guided me into a waiting room. As we walked down the narrow hallway SGT Adams explained some of the procedures and activities planned for today's Memorial Ceremony. While I was waiting, a tall middle aged woman hurried in and announced to Sergeant Adams that she was Mrs. Jean Fedigan and she was there to represent Sister Jose at Jimmie's Memorial Ceremony. He paused for a moment, not knowing what to say, and then calmly asked Mrs. Fedigan if she had her confirmation letter from the Casualty Office. At her negative reply, you could see the tension in SGT Adams shoulders disappear.

Mrs. Fedigan had been the private secretary to Sister Jose for a while at the Tucson Convent. After consulting with Monsignor Cahalane she came to Arlington for the Memorial Ceremony, feeling that Sister Jose needed to be "represented." Excusing himself for a moment, SGT Adams walked over to me and quietly asked me if I knew anything about this. I told him it was the first I had heard of the situation but I had no problem with Mrs. Fedigan being present. At that point, he diplomatically introduced Jean Fedigan to me as "the designated representative for Sister Jose."

Apparently Mrs. Fedigan was not very pleased with the situation and demanded that I send a copy of all the paperwork to her home and a copy to Monsignor Cahalane in Tucson. For the rest of the morning she sat quietly, observing and listening intently as the various cemetery representatives quietly spoke with me and explained the various procedures and activities. Before we could leave for the Memorial Ceremony, another clerk walked into the room and placed a stack of forms in front of me to sign, quietly explaining the purpose of the form as he turned over each page with diligent care.

We were led outside to a waiting limousine. Offering Mrs. Fedigan the back seat, I chose to sit up front next to the driver. Slowly the limo moved forward following the symbolic hearse out to the gravesite. The Flag Team & Rifle teams were already in place near the gravesite, awaiting our arrival. The limousine slowly passed out the main gate, crossed over a city street, and re-entered the cemetery through another wrought iron gate. Then we carefully navigated our way through narrow tree lined avenues until we reached an area designated for Korean War veterans. Upon our arrival at the designated hillside, a young Airman reverently directed us to stand on one side of the path.

There had been a few raindrops on the windshield as we drove up the tree lined lane but now the clouds had begun to thin out. Meanwhile the Air Force Flag Team stepped to the rear of the hearse in a silent cadence, and slowly unrolled the American Flag. The flag would symbolize the missing coffin for A1C Jimmie Hobday. Placing my Disabled American Veterans hat on my head as I watched the Flag Team and falling into step behind them as they headed for the gravesite. Mrs. Fedigan paced a few steps behind me.

An Air Force Funeral Affairs representative walking to the left of the procession, kept pace with the Flag Team. They solemnly marched in a slow timed cadence, the clik-clak of their footsteps barely audible on the gravel. In contrast, the plastic wheels on my folding walker clattered loudly as I pushed it along. The camera bag and a raincoat were hung across the front of the walker for easy access. The sounds of birds and chattering insects mixed with the aroma of the morning's rain called for my attention.

At the gravesite, the Flag Team, still holding the outstretched flag, stood in front of the headstone which was already in place. A small American flag placed next to the gravestone, gently waved in the breeze. Mrs. Fedigan and I were ushered to a set of folding seats placed near the side of the gravesite as a Mortuary Affairs representative spoke in a hushed voice further explaining the program. In a hushed voice he introduced us to the Air Force Chaplain-Priest, Padre McGuill who would be performing the service. Just before Padre McGuill began to speak, the sun shone brightly on the cemetery. The bright sunlight caused wisps of steam to rise off the asphalt road nearby. I already had beads of sweat underneath that dark suit and quietly dabbed my forehead with a handkerchief as sweat began to form in large drops.

"Today we are remembering of Jimmie, the good in his life. Please accept the sympathy, the love, the prayers, the honors, and the gratitude of Jimmie's country for his service in the Air Force." As the Priest spoke, a bell tolled softly in the background. Mrs. Fedigan was sitting next to me and she kept turning around trying to identify where the sounds were coming from. The Priest continued, "We especially thank you for remembering him all these years and know that now in this hallowed space, this sacred ground, he is finally at rest."

Just before Padre McGuill finished his Eulogy, a flight of jets flew over in the traditional missing man formation. I had held it together until that moment! Tear drops moistened my eyes. The Air Force accepted and recognized me as Jimmie's son, but now I had the honor of being at Arlington while recognition of his ultimate sacrifice was officially and finally bestowed on him by a grateful nation for all eternity to see.

As the Padre ended his comments with the Lord's Prayer, the Rifle Team fired a twenty-one gun salute in three measured volleys. A lone soldier on the hill behind us began to softly play Taps on his bugle. The Flag Team prepared to fold the flag. The absolute silence broken only by the lonely wail of a police siren in the distance as the soldiers slowly and methodically folded the Burial Flag. Taking the flag from the Team, the Captain of the Flag Team knelt on the grass in front of me "On behalf of the President of the United States and the Air Force I present this flag to you as a token of our condolences . . ." The Flag Team & Rifle Team then reformed and slowly, somberly marched off to their waiting vehicle.

Using my digital camera, they took a couple of photos of me standing by Jimmie's headstone and with the Presentation Case. The Funeral Services Office would mail the oversized Case to me later in the week so it wouldn't have to be carried on the plane. The hinged triangular Presentation Case was solid walnut, the folded

Burial Flag fit tightly into one side of it and the other side had a ribbon bar with Jimmie's awards and a nametag. A Funeral Services Representative guided Mrs. Fedigan and me toward the waiting limousine that would return us to the visitor's center. The aroma of the cherry trees mixed with the scent of cut grass and just a hint of rain, leaving a sweet smell in the summer air. Suddenly I was aware of birds singing in the trees around us.

The Casualty Office Representative, Mr. Jamison, approached and quietly thanked Mrs. Fedigan as he walked with us back to the limousine. Mrs. Fedigan got out at the visitor's center and said goodbye in a subdued voice. As the car door closed, Jamison turned and asked, "She did not know about your status?" Smiling I replied "No! I didn't want to bring it up to a stranger. I appreciate your discretion on this matter." As we drove through the big wrought iron gates at the edge of the Cemetery, he said, "You would be surprised, your situation isn't that uncommon so we are used to it. Is there somewhere you need to go before I drop you at the subway Metro station?"

"Yes, I had promised a friend to leave a gift by her brother's name on the Viet Nam Wall. Would that be out of the way?" "No problem, it's just a few blocks away." Jamison drove me to the Wall, parking the sedan near one of the entrances, and waited for me as I navigated the folding walker down that long brick sidewalk amongst all of the people that had lined up to pay their respects. The Viet Nam Wall Memorial was always crowded very day of the year, despite the weather. For something that had initially been very controversial, it had become a very special place for all visitors to Washington D.C.

That ground is so hallowed. Conversation naturally shifts to a whisper as the sidewalk approaches the tall black marble columns. Even the street noise from the surrounding city seems to disappear. People tend to walk softly and avoid eye contact as they view the thousands of names etched into the stone columns. If the light is just right, you can often see a teardrop in the eye of the most hardened soul. Placing the memento & card at the base of column number 32, I noticed that the reflections of people standing around me appeared as ghostly images looking back at us.

Upon my return to the curb and slipping into the back seat of the limousine, it felt as though a great burden was gently lifted off my shoulders. I felt relieved, peaceful, and happy inside. Mr. Jamison must have felt it too as he made light conversation as he navigated the limousine through the congested streets towards the Metro station. The ten-minute ride to Washington National Airport on the subway was hardly enough time to sort through my bag and make sure I had everything in order. The sky had cleared up; the summer sun was hot and strong as I rode the escalator into the air terminal. The dark suit was too hot for this humid weather! The plane didn't leave until 5p.m. so I had time for a good lunch at the restaurant and maybe a short nap after I changed back into my traveling clothes.

However, I was too excited to sleep so I quickly changed, repacked my bag, and checked the flight status board. While at Arlington National Cemetery, I had carefully turned on a digital recorder tucked into my coat pocket when the Memorial Ceremony started. I wanted to remember as much as possible about this day. The pocket recorder was useful backup, since taking pictures during the actual Memorial Ceremony wasn't permitted. Finding a quiet corner near the loading gate I bravely began to listen to the recording as I sat waiting for the boarding call. My eyes filled with tears as I listened to the Padre's voice once again.

Despite being exhausted and my legs hurting from all of the walking, I could not go to sleep on the plane. The electric scooter would have been a better choice than the folding walker! I have always loved plane rides and found them relaxing, so usually I can fall fast asleep as soon as we lift off, but not today! The window seat I was in must have recently had a new window installed because the plastic was exceptionally clear. I busied myself by taking pictures of the cloud formations as we neared thirty thousand feet in altitude and then made a few notes on the day's activities. Finally, a quick nap shortly before we began our decent into Denver.

We landed in Denver at 6pm so by the time the twelve-passenger shuttle bus arrived at the hotel it was almost eight o'clock and I was very tired. Grabbing a quick dinner before the dining room closed I went up to my room, showered and set up my bag and clothes for the final portion of the trip back to Arizona early in the morning. Spending a few moments laying in bed going over my notes from the trip I fell asleep, the notebook still in my hand.

My head was a bit groggy when the alarm went off the next morning and I was thankful I'd packed everything the night before. Hurriedly dressing, I gulped down two cups of coffee from the courtesy pot, grabbed my bag, and headed for the lobby. Another cup of coffee and a donut in the lobby was just enough to help me stay awake for the forty-five-minute ride to the airport. Fortunately, I had enough time to eat a plate of scrambled eggs with pancakes at the food court before boarding the plane for the return flight home.

The plane was passing over a small rugged mountain range as we crossed into Arizona. Pulling out a notepad, I wrote a letter to Jimmie Hobday, the father I never really had a chance to know. I started out by telling the story of our lives together and ended it as though he was sitting in front of me and we were talking.

"Dad, if I ever find anyone that knew you, I would like him to be able to tell me about you. Your likes and dislikes. A funny story or two, and even a little bit about your short military life, and hopefully they will find a photo or two from a scrapbook.

Did you ever tell your friends about me? Did you tell your brother & sister or friends, the real story about my birth and my mother? I look at your photo and try to imagine you as the dad I could have had. I think you would have been a very kind and gentle father. Your voice, your face, forever etched into my memory as a child, were always comforting. I have your photo with the B-29 crew, right above my own Army retirement photo on the wall next to my bed. I carry a snapshot of you in my wallet. Rest in Peace dad, your loving son, Dane"

EPILOGUE

Twelve months after the Memorial Ceremony at Arlington National Cemetery for Jimmie Hobday, I moved out of assisted care at Grayson House and re-entered what I call "real life." Staying with a friend for several months near Prescott Valley provided the opportunity to loose twenty pounds of excess weight and to decide what I wanted for the future. Though there was a lot of pain involved, as my body was still slowly healing and gaining strength, I began to relish each day's labor. Physical tasks were being accomplished that were impossible for me during the last few years. I was actually enjoying simple household chores and doing light work in the yard despite pain every night. Unused muscles screamed in agony yet I continued pushing myself mentally and physically every day.

Eventually I rented a small home in a rural area outside Prescott which forced me to push myself even harder just trying to do the simple upkeep things around the house and yard. The VA doctor allowed me to reduce some medications as my body steadily gained strength. I will always be dependent on a heavy daily dose of medications, but they allow me independence. The alternative would be to return to assisted care and I don't want to go back to that type of living environment. Dosages on some of those meds may be lowered in the future as my body changes. The various pains and problems associated with my injuries will always plague me for the rest of my life but I won't allow that to stop me from doing as much as possible.

However, the quality of life is rapidly improving. For a short while, I can enjoy life again in a "normal" way. Buying a home, having friends to socialize with and even starting to date for the first time in years, each one a new adventure. Life is getting better and I can look forward to the future. For the first time in years I have the energy and desire to create a new life for myself and possibly do a few things differently.

Every time I see Doctor Newman, the primary care physician at the Veteran's Hospital in Prescott, she is constantly amazed at the almost perfect lab results and my stubborn refusal to allow myself to stagnate. With her support and encouragement I continue to physically improve. Once again, though limited to some degree, I can enjoy my favorite past times of travel, camping and exploring. I had turned in my driver's license right before I went into the Sedona nursing home and have never renewed it, as I don't want to chance causing an accident because of my slowed reflexes and poor vision.

I have learned to rely on others or to find alternative methods for solving transportation needs. The travel scooter & power chair still provide excellent local transportation with friends taking me into town once or twice a month for groceries and shopping. Acquiring a hot tub spa has played a large role in easing pain & discomfort while being able to reduce the amount of daily medications that I must consume. By using the spa three or four times a day, there is less need for some of the pain and muscle spasm medications. Surprisingly I am comfortable living away from the city and not having a vehicle of my own or being around many people.

On the 25th of March 2010 an unexpected letter arrived from Anthony Mora, one of the Chosin Few Association members. Mr.

Mora had been part of the mass mailings in the attempt to gain support and participation in the Memorial Ceremony for John Spruell. He had never responded to my invitation as the letter had been misplaced, and recently Mr. Mora found my original letter amongst his papers.

Mr. Mora wrote me a two page letter on two 6"x8" pages. His strong handwriting, difficult to read at times, provided additional information on The Battle of Chosin and the fate of John Spruell.

" . . . I was Security Platoon Squad Leader for 'B' Btry, 57th Field Artillery Battalion. Since we stayed on the perimeter, I only saw CPL Spruell a few times. Though injured, I made my way back on foot close to Hagaru-ri and was picked up by an army tank and evacuated to a hospital ship for surgery. I spent eight months in Letterman Army Hospital in San Francisco. I was also listed as Missing in Action for a few days after I was injured and losing my squad. They had all died so I was the only survivor . . . When I received your letter, I really wanted to go but I couldn't because of medical reasons, then your letter was misplaced. I had two or three hospitalizations, the last one being for heart surgery. I am in good health now.

I was cleaning out my office files and found your letter; sorry this reply is so late. The Chosin Few Veterans Group is having a reunion in Little Rock, Arkansas on May 19th through the 23rd and as the family and friends of CPL Spruell you would be welcome to attend . . . There was a DVD made of persons who were in the Breakout of the Chosin Reservoir and they used some of us in it. A full length movie is also being made for the big theatres . . . I am very proud to have been a comrade of CPL Spruell and very sorry he didn't make it back. The memory of CPL Spruell should be of Honor, Glory, and Pride. I don't know where Cortez (Colorado) is, but if you have any reunions to honor CPL Spruell I know I would want to be there if the Lord lets me. I have many memories of B Battery and would like to share them with CPL Spruell's relatives and friends. Anthony T. Mora."

Sitting down that afternoon I typed out a reply to Mr. Mora and forwarded a copy of everything to Dennis Spruell in Cortez.

"Mr. Mora,

What a fantastic surprise to get your letter! As you can see by the address I have moved and was very fortunate that someone at the old address took the time and hand carried your letter to me. Your little bit of information and the fact you were in contact with CPL Spruell just adds something special for the family that we did not have before.

The Memorial Ceremony that was held in Cortez for John Spruell had a larger attendance than expected. The Ceremony was done in an honorable & professional fashion so that all Chosin/ Hagaru-ri survivors and dead were properly honored. Unfortunately most of the survivors that I had been able to contact either had prior engagements or were too ill to travel, just as you were.

I saw the documentary you mentioned and thought it was very good, including your interview. I hope that the movie will be just as factual also and I look forward to seeing it. I am sending you a copy of the Eulogy that I gave at the Memorial Ceremony for John and am sending a copy of your letter to the surviving members of the Spruell family. They may contact you after reading the letter.

I would be honored to attend the 57th/Chosin Few reunion but I have just bought a fix-up house and am in the middle of extensive remodeling so I will not be able to attend the reunion. Perhaps I will be able to go to the next one! I would like to share something special with you Mr. Mora that relates to CPL Spruell and you. One of John Spruell's high school friends was Jimmie Hobday, my birth father. John Spruell had enlisted while in high school but my dad went on to college.

It seems that John's death at Hagaru-ri played some part in my dad giving up a college scholarship and joining the Air Force. Later, as a B-29 tail gunner, he was shot down and killed during a bombing raid over Suiho, Korea on 13 September 1952. This last July I had the honor to fly to Arlington National Cemetery for a Memorial Ceremony for my dad.

After all these years both men have finally been given due honors and symbolically laid to rest. None of this would have been possible if it had not been for the help we received from many of the Chosin Few survivors over the last two years as well as many other veterans! We are truly a small community within ourselves. That old phrase "soldiers helping soldiers" says a lot! Perhaps you and I will meet someday and you might even have a chance to meet some of the Spruell family too. Sincerely, Dane Hobday Hays"

It should be noted that Dennis Spruell left his undercover police position in Cortez last year, and returned to uniformed duty. Dennis was recently elected as the Police Chief for Cortez, Colorado. Last year additional military reports were finally declassified and the tragedy of Chosin is still unfolding. Two more men have been located that were members of the 57th Field Artillery Battalion, though neither of them remembers ever meeting John Spruell.

Chuck Haley and his wife Marilyn have become close friends also. We maintain contact by email and the occasional phone call. Their support and positive attitude over these last couple of years has meant a lot to me. I plan to return to Cortez soon to visit and of course to stop by the cemetery. The City of Cortez, Colorado remains very special to me. For the first time in my life I'm proud to call a place my hometown! There is a strong possibility that I may move to Cortez in a couple of years and stay there for the rest of my life.

Time and circumstances create such a variety of changes in our lives. When I was younger I would listen to older folks talk about their lives and think, "How can they have done all those things?" Now I know! Many friends have come and gone over the years, but the acquaintances that I made in Cortez and several people from the various veterans' organizations have kept in contact with me on a regular basis. Some of them like Jim Westendorf pay frequent visits to the gravesite of John Spruell in Cortez. Quite often he will send me a photograph of John Spruell's gravestone as the seasons change. He placed a military "challenge coin" on the gravestone over a year ago and it's still there!

There was never a reply from Mrs. Fedigan or Monsignor Cahalane after I sent them copies of the Arlington National Cemetery paperwork. Occasionally I think about sending them a second letter, telling them of my relationship to Sister Jose and Jimmie, but I never took the time to do so. A few months ago I finally called Mrs. Fedigan and spoke with her for about fifteen minutes on the telephone. She was apprehensive and very cautious in her remarks to me as I revealed my relationship to Sister Jose. Apparently Sister Jose had never discussed her life in Cortez, her brothers or anything about their lives. Sister Jose remains an enigma, even after her death. She was a skilled, accomplished, intelligent, and dedicated woman, totally absorbed in the lives of others not so fortunate. Yet Sister Jose never allowed herself to have a life beyond service to the Church. Perhaps it is better for some things not to be said! If they read this book then I am sure they will understand.

Mother is still alive and in a nursing home near Phoenix. Her schizophrenia and the dementia caused by age still control her life and make it difficult for anyone to be her friend. One moment I am her "little angel" and the next "the devil" so I have not visited or spoken with her since that day in 2008. Because she lost all of her savings and the money from father's insurance policy she is now completely dependent on State & Federal aid to cover her needs. Several businesses, including two nursing homes, have given up their attempts to collect on fraudulent checks she wrote or obligations left unpaid. It has taken almost three years to shake loose and solve some of the legal problems mother created. Amongst them are six different persons that mother gave full Powers of Attorney to, without rescinding or notifying any of the other individuals, which has created quite a legal quagmire! There is a slim possibility she will be taken care of by a court appointed guardian, once we can cut through some additional red tape and get all parties working together.

Due to administrative glitches caused by her interference over the years, providing proper care for my mother has not always been easy. However there is still a lot of work ahead of us to correct some of the problems she created for herself because of the mental illness and through her own misguided actions. If my father had signed her up for Social Security Disability in the 1970s and allowed her to receive counseling and better medical care she might be in better shape today. Mother's younger sister Sarah, occasionally asks about her but that is the extent of the interest in mother's wellbeing. I don't think those burned bridges will never be repaired! A social worker and an attorney keep me updated on mother's condition. Due to her vitriolic nature and my limited transportation, I don't expect that I will ever pay my mother another visit!

Little Pooh has blossomed into a well behaved dog that is a wonderful companion. Pooh can never replace Buzz though she is just as loyal, protective, and loving. Because of her natural abilities and the training she has been given since I adopted her, Pooh & I were invited to participate with over 50 school-trained Service Dogs as "companions" to the contestants in the Northern Arizona Special Olympics for the last two years. Like Buzz, she takes each new adventure in stride and has even learned how to play and get along with children and to socialize with other dogs. Sadly she never learned how to just play as a dog, so simple games of chase, tug-of-war and others are still foreign to her. Though recently she has discovered that running around the yard can be fun and she now sings for her dinner.

Pooh fell in love with camping and boating on her very first trip. She has her own sleeping bag and enjoys exploring the wilderness or riding in the boat. When I'm ready to take her on our daily walk through the neighborhood she jumps for joy and gives a short howl of pleasure. The stories of Buzz & Pooh attracted the attention of the publisher of two regional pet magazines and a couple of articles were written about us. Recently I was asked to join one of the magazines as a contributing writer which will keep me busy.

Someone once said that time heals all wounds. Perhaps it does, though we always seem to hold onto our pains and illnesses as though they were buried treasure. It appears that despite age and many medical problems Fred Parker has also managed to overcome tremendous odds over the last several years and is doing fine now. Bud Farrell and his wife were able to visit Fred during their vacation this year, almost 59 years to the day since Fred was shot down over Korea. Apparently it was quite an emotional reunion. Perhaps someday in the future I will have the chance to meet the two men in person.

Bud has become a close friend and confidant, often giving me good advice on this story or encouraging me when I become frustrated. When Bud sent me the first draft of his Foreword for this book, I had chills down my spine when I read it for the first time. For now, it is comforting to know that Fred is doing better and if we do have the chance to meet perhaps Fred will be able to tell me a little bit more about my dad. I'm continuing the Korean War research, the possibility exists that I may still find someone else that knew Jimmie Hobday and John Spruell.

Doctor Nagy and his wife Peggy have become my best friends over the last couple of years. We try to go camping or boating as often as possible during the summer months and sometimes in the winter I ride on the back of his motorcycle for short trips. Frank is now semi-retired from his medical practice so finally he has more time for play after a long and highly successful career. He just turned 70, but he looks and acts as though he was much younger. Without his help and intervention when I was misdiagnosed and placed in the Sedona nursing home I wouldn't be here today! Just think of the many people that could benefit from health care professionals who give a few moments of extra effort and time to solving a problem! Just like the Army Reservist doctors and nurses at the Fort Hood hospital. Their dedication and efforts are another reason I am alive today.

My life has been packed with many experiences and at times it's been quite exciting and unpredictable, far exceeding my childhood dreams and expectations. During high school I had often said I wanted to go to college, travel the world, and meet famous people. Not having the faintest clue how I was going to achieve such lofty objectives. Unintentionally, despite many obstacles mixed my own stubbornness, I succeeded in achieving those dreams and goals! Of course, there are always some small regrets or 'what ifs' in everyone's life, but over all I am content and happy with the way everything has turned out. No longer feeling like an old man on his death bed, I look forward to each day and new adventures. Thanking God for a second chance. Life is too precious to waste, just sitting around waiting for something to happen.

Gone are the nightmares and feelings of hopelessness and frustration from earlier years. There is no more guilt or anguish over issues from my childhood or my military injuries. The accomplishments in life definitely outweigh the defeats and I wouldn't change a thing. I still require a large amount of medication on a daily basis and live with constant pain but that is a small price to pay. Of course I have to be careful how much physical activity I do but at least for a while I am out of the mobility chair, and don't even have to use a cane now. The VA doctors tells me that I may have several years before I must return to the motorized chair and that I should enjoy my life to the fullest, continuing to challenge myself physically and mentally. I may be retired and disabled but it doesn't mean I have to sit back and play invalid!

These last twenty-two years since I was medically retired were just as hectic and eventful as the previous forty-three years of my life. I was presented with an unusual opportunity when I was injured and forced to retire. Sometimes you need a wakeup call such as a life changing event to make you realize just how priceless life is, and the need to make every minute in your life count. It is never too late to change your way of life, your job, or to challenge yourself to achieve or overcome a handicap.

There are many more stories that I could tell, all true. My advice to anyone would be the simple statement from Kirk Douglas when I was ten years old: "Never Give Up On Your Dreams!" Perhaps there is still more to come, I certainly hope so. Only time will tell. My greatest pleasure each day is to work a bit in the yard or take my dog for an early morning walk. She treats each day as a new adventure and so do I. Maybe next year I will take an ocean cruise, last summer I started learning how to kayak and this year . . . well who knows!